W9-BYP-560

DAVID A. LICHTER

A Great Treasury
of
Christian Spirituality

EX LIBRIS
DAVID A. LIGHTER

A Great Treasury
of
Christian Spirituality

Classic Readings in the Life of Faith
and the Love of God

Compiled by
Edward Alcott

CARILLON  BOOKS
1978

A GREAT TREASURY
OF CHRISTIAN SPIRITUALITY

A Carillon Book
Carillon Books Edition published 1978
ISBN: 0-89310-039-0 (hard cover)
ISBN: 0-89310-040-4 (paperback)
Library of Congress Catalog Card Number: 78-59319
Copyright © 1978 by Carillon Books
All Rights Reserved
Printed in the United States of America

CARILLON BOOKS
2115 Summit Avenue
St. Paul, Minnesota 55105

CONTENTS

FOREWORD

What is Christian spirituality? Christian spirituality is simply the growth process in the life of faith and love of God. It is initiated by responding to God in faith and terminates only in the complete possession of God in the life to come. Thus, Christian spirituality includes the whole journey in the growth of faith from simple belief in God to the attainment of salvation itself. However, even on this earthly plane, the maturing of the life of faith brings forth profound experiences of the love of God. These experiences are called mystical because they happen independently of the senses and thus defy reason. Mystical experiences are in the realm of spiritual intuition. They "deify" man in the sense that in the moments of experiential union with God, both God and man become one in spirit. Mystical union is not the end of the spiritual life but simply an advanced degree of the sanctification process. These experiences are foretastes of heavenly joy and peace that will ultimately be given to all who abide in God. Indeed, all men of faith are mystics in embryo. But it is through deepened discipleship with Christ that the life of faith bursts forth into deep degrees of communion with the love of God Himself.

One of the most fascinating aspects of Christianity is the essential unity of Protestant and Catholic thought on spiritual growth. This is reassuring, especially in an age of institutional change, authority crisis and religious turmoil. Church ceremonies may change, Christian doctrines evolve and differing Christian sects appear, but the process of one's sanctification through spiritual growth remains the same.

It is the purpose of these readings to allow the reader to perceive for himself the continuity of the teachings of the great spiritual writers on the growth process entailed in spirituality. The three themes of these readings demonstrate the progressive degrees of the development of spiritual growth called sanctification. One initiates the Christian path by faith, progresses through discipleship and culminates the earthly sojourn in mystic union with God. Each selection focuses on the teachings of ancient, medieval and modern writers on a topic of spiritual growth, thereby enabling the reader to perceive the historical unity in the teaching of spiritual direction.

One should be aware of the distinctions between salvation and sanctification in the life of Christian spirituality. St. Paul tells us that salvation is a gift. He says: "... no man is put right in God's sight by doing what the law requires; what the law does is to make man know that he has sinned ... all men have sinned and are far away from God's saving presence. But by the free gift of God's grace they are all put right with him through Christ Jesus, who sets them free."[1] Indeed, through Christ's redemption, God has accomplished everything for man. What one must do is accept this gift in trusting faith. Yet it is not easy for man to operate in the faith dimension. For at times he must crucify his intellect to believe what he cannot see. As man in Adam walked away from God in pride, now he must retrace those steps in humble faith. Rational thought can take one only to the abyss of faith. To leap in darkness or to remain stationary is the crucial dilemma of existence.

The absolute minimum of the Christian spiritual life is the belief that Jesus is savior and that salvation is freely given to those who humbly recognize their need for it. However, when man takes this leap of faith, he becomes possessed by the Holy Spirit to do the will of God, not out of a sense of obligation but out of an overwhelming feeling of gratitude for what God has done for him in Christ.

This response to the motivating influence of the Holy Spirit is the sanctification process. Faith not only grants salvation but also initiates the spiritual journey of sanctification. It is the work of the Holy Spirit to sanctify the believer and bring about joy and peace as the normal life of the Christian. To the degree that one responds to his sanctification is the degree that one opens himself to a fuller spiritual life in God. Accepting Christ as savior takes but a moment, but to grow in the spiritual life takes a lifetime.

Although one will be saved through a life of repentance and belief, he nevertheless relinquishes the here and now effects of his salvation, if he does not respond to the sanctifying promptings of the Holy Spirit. The results of Redemption are to transform the individual into participation in the love of God in this life, as well as to a more profound degree in the next. Consequently, sin seriously retards this experiential fellowship.

---

1. I Rom.: 20-24.

One who does grow in discipleship with Christ is first crucified in a purification process sometimes called purgation. Purgation is the work of the Holy Spirit, to mature man from his fallen egocentric human nature so that he might discover his true image which is the reflection of God. Selflessness is to replace selfishness; compassion is to replace arrogance. Yet maturity is a difficult road beset with all the problems of a fallen egocentric nature. The Holy Spirit constantly prods the man of faith to surrender his baser nature to that of spiritual liberation. This crucifixion precedes resurrection. The Holy Spirit is likened to Francis Thompson's "The Hound of Heaven," Who, as a hound, continually trails at man's heels until he surrenders to his transformation. For as soon as the Holy Spirit enters the human spirit, He requires one to leave his former master of sin and be subject to the divine will. As man's fallen nature focuses all things upon self, spiritual life centers all upon Christ. The ego wishes to lead man to sin, but spiritual life longs to lead him to righteousness and mystic communion.

If a Christian remains in a carnal condition long after experiencing his new birth in faith, he hinders God's salvation from realizing its full experiential potential. Only when he is responding to grace, constantly governed by the Holy Spirit, can the fruits of salvation be manifested in him. Yet this growing in grace causes conflict. This is spiritual warfare. Oftentimes believers doubt whether they have faith or even despair of spiritual growth thinking they are just too bad. Yet the very fact that there is contention is a sign of faith. The way of purgation is the way of the cross. It is the way of wisdom, for it deepens one's faith. God can only give to those who believe and respond. When man asks for forgiveness and regeneration, God surely bestows it. But it is through conflict with his fallen nature that God induces the believer to seek and grasp the total triumph of sanctified liberation that Christ has won for him.

One learns through many failures that true fulfillment can be found only in Christ. By refusing to despair, persevering in prayer and rejecting egocentric love, one waits to be discovered by the transforming encounter of mystical experience. Indeed, there is purgation before the mystical birth and purgations following in the continuous sanctification process. Purgations continuous with the mystical life are hence called the "Dark Night" of the Soul. The first series of mystical experiences strengthen the believer to progress deeper in the life of sanctification. Spiritual writers affirm the need of experiencing God in some profound degree before one is enabled to progress deeply in self-surrender.

Although many people are repelled at the suffering involved in mystical purgations, the mystics rejoice, believing enlightenment, though painful, is of more consequence than blissful ignorance. Indeed, the sufferings are nothing more than developing human and thus spiritual maturity. The growth is much the same as the child learning to walk through many falls and cuts. All human life is a combination of joy and pain. So, too, is the life of sanctification, although its joys and sorrows are more acutely felt because of the deeper degree of spiritual perception. The mystics parallel the "Dark Night" to the Biblical injunction: "I chastise those whom I love" (Rev. 3:19). They interpret this as meaning that God purifies those who come to him in discipleship through Christ. William Johnston explains the "Dark Night" as follows:

> At first the consolation of love predominates; but this will usually give way to pain, for one thing, the stirring of love is unifying; it is . . . a "one-ing exercise," in which the scattered faculties are withdrawn from their attachment to created things and fixed upon God. And this unification of the whole personality—gradually being united in itself and united with God—cannot but bring anguish: suspended in anguish between God (for He is surrounded by a thick cloud of unknowing) or created things (for they are buried beneath a thick cloud of forgetting). And so suspended in isolated anguish, the soul has only its painful love crying out pitifully to God whom it cannot know or see.[2]

The mystics believe that God can never be perfectly present to man here below on account of the human condition, but He can seem to be almost perfectly absent in extreme affliction. That was Christ's suffering on the cross: "My God, my God, why hast thou forsaken me." Simone Weil, a twentieth-century mystic, maintains that in this time of suffering the soul must remember that love is a direction and not an emotional state. Thus the desire for God is in itself love though there is no

2. Wm. Johnston, *The Stillpoint,* p. 33-4. New York: Fordham U. Press, 1970.

emotional feeling. The soul has to go on wanting to love though it may be with an infinitesimal part of itself.[3] Then, as Scripture says, those who wait upon the Lord shall not be forsaken.

Why must a soul pass through such purification? St. Teresa of Avila says: "Real love must be pure and generous. This is the crucible in which souls are proved. In order to give herself completely to God, the soul must be convinced of the nothingness of the world and the deceit of all things which do not lead to God. Convinced of this, she will seek the Beloved, the one and only font of all beauty and goodness."[4] The Protestant philosopher, Sören Kierkegaard, says much the same: "Suffering is at once the God-given grace of the only way which leads to a deepening relationship with God . . . and the God-task of following the way by which, in an ethico-religious manner we, as believers, are to learn what we must learn from Christ . . . So long as consciousness of sin has not taken the form of suffering, one does not yet truly feel the need for redemption."[5]

Perseverance in the "Dark Night" results in the fullness of the mystical life. This fullness is called "illumination" or ecstatic union. Illumination is not the end of the spiritual life but a progression within it. This is the time when God ravishes the soul with his gifts of joy, love, and peace. The soul is ecstatic in its absorption in the divine. The body seems abandoned and the senses are suspended while the soul transcends the sphere of its natural operations and participates in supernatural life. St. Paul indicates this absorption when he says his ecstasy was such that he did not know whether he was in his body or out of the body. St. Teresa says that God unites Himself with the soul in such a way that none can understand it save God and the soul, and even the soul afterwards cannot explain it. The graces of illumination are not habitual but transitory. They usher in the maturity of the mystical state. The soul is once again refreshed to complete the final donation of its spirit and will to God. Once again mystical joy gives way to spiritual aridity. However, continuing perseverance in the "Dark Night" culminates in an unchanging peace. "There in the very depths of the soul," says St. Teresa, "the soul enjoys the

3. Simone Weil, *Waiting on God*, p. 80. New York: G.P. Putnam's Sons, 1951.

4. Fr. Thomas (ed.), *St. Teresa of Avila*, p. 158-60. Westminster, Maryland: Newman, 1963.

5. Louis Dupre, *Kierkegaard as Theologian*, p. 88-90. New York: Sheed & Ward, 1963.

presence of the Beloved (God), in the midst of a great silence. Here the soul is and remains in union with its God."[6] It is a pale anticipation of the eternal day of beatific vision. It is, perhaps, the closest union possible for man to attain with God on earth.

Every man is called to journey back to God in faith. The mystical life is nothing other than the approaching end of the spiritual journey. God is now in sight for blind faith has given way to the certainty of God's being and man's destiny in him. Mystical insights are given to man in order that he conform his will to the maximum demands of faith and love. Mystical knowledge reveals the illusions of man's permanent satisfaction in anything but the divine. The mystical process is painful though steeped in truth. Its reward is personal fulfillment already realized, if only partially and in passing in this life.

In conclusion, the purpose of these readings is to reveal the Christian-becoming-process as viewed by some of the great teachers of spirituality throughout the Ages. The whole journey of spiritual growth is given from the moment of faith to mystical union. Although salvation is a free gift of God, man's response to this gift transforms life even in the human dimension to experience existentially some of the joys of the life to come.

6. Thomas, *op. cit.* p. 182.

The Approach to God

Part I

THE APPROACH TO GOD

Since the scientific revolution of the seventeenth century, modern man questions as never before the existence of the supernatural. Contemporary man bases so much of his belief on a rational, ordered universe that he questions the super-rational or spiritual as perhaps superstitions. Consequently, our modern culture creates a climate in which it is more difficult to believe.

A book of this nature, therefore, must treat the difficulties of belief before beginning the process of spirituality. To believe or not to believe is an important religious problem of our time. Christianity suffered greatly in the nineteenth century with Marx calling religion the opiate of the people, Freud asserting belief as the result of guilt feelings and Darwin discounting the hitherto accepted literal belief of the creation story. Rationalism, indeed, reached its zenith in the last quarter of the nineteenth century but such smugness vanished abruptly with the holocaust of World War I. The post-war intellectual climate of existential philosophy once again opened the inquiry of belief to the intellectual. Gabriel Marcel and Martin Buber represent the best of these God existentialists. Antecedent to this philosophic quest was the revival of interest in mysticism as an experiential argument for the existence of God. At the turn of the century, Evelyn Underhill, Friedrich von Hugel and William James gathered and published accounts of the mystics throughout the history of the Christian era. The result was a popular and even a devotional interest in this spirituality. Today interest in spirituality has grown phenomenally.

The first two selections in the present compilation deal with the problem of belief. Illtyd Trethowan in his book *The Basis of Belief* analyzes the limitations of logic in trying to prove God's existence. Paul Tillich in *Dynamics of Faith* analyzes faith as ultimate concern and contrasts faith and doubt.

Belief and Unbelief

The next series of selections presuppose the decision for faith has been made or is in the making. Notice the emphasis placed upon prayer in the following selections. Gabriel Marcel, a Christian existentialist, discusses what is prayer and relates it to the quality of interpersonal dialogue. St. Bonaventure, an early Franciscan, states nothing is accomplished without divine aid. But grace comes to those who seek it from their hearts humbly and devoutly. Dietrich Bonhoeffer, a Lutheran pastor, believes that only those who obey believe. Indeed, Bonhoeffer died in Nazi Germany for his beliefs. A Renaissance Englishman, Walter Hilton, sees the first great obstacle in the spiritual life as pride, "unless one sees he will not believe," while the second obstacle is in the will, to respond to the faith one believes. St. Teresa, the only female doctor of the church, emphatically states that without prayer the soul is paralyzed for spiritual growth. Augustine Baker, a seventeenth century English monk, stresses the necessity of strong motivation to persevere in the spiritual life. Lastly, Sören Kierkegaard, a nineteenth century Lutheran philosopher-theologian, believes that it is only through dying to one's baser self that one rises in spiritual maturity.

Each of these writers is an acknowledged giant in the field of spirituality. It is left to the reader to analyze the thoughts of these writers. Do they basically agree or disagree with each other in the process of spiritual growth?

THE BASIS OF BELIEF*
By Illtyd Trethowan

This selection is taken from the above book which won the 1958 award by the Thomas More Association for the most distinguished contribution of that year to Catholicism. "In these pages the author creates a new approach to a philosophy of religion which is particularly advantageous because 'it does not require an array of technical terms, metaphysical notions and piled-up syllogisms . . . . The philosophy of religion, in the form in which it will be recommended here, is not a way of complicating religion for believers; it is concerned principally with unbelievers and endeavors to hold that the removal of such obstacles is the chief duty of charity laid upon Christians today.' " Illtyd Trethowan is a Benedictine monk who takes issue with those who would like to prove the existence of God by reason. He shows forth here the limits of such an approach.

THE "PROOFS" IN PRACTICE

The importance of resisting syllogistic proofs of God's existence should be obvious enough in a general way. Bad arguments are very effective in turning people away from religion. They suppose that, when they have exposed the flaw in a syllogistic "proof," they are entitled to dismiss the topic of God's existence altogether, and Catholic apologists seem sometimes almost to encourage them to take this line. What is not perhaps commonly recognized is that people who believe in God are sometimes deterred from becoming Catholics by conventional presentations of the "proofs." They suppose—they may even be given to understand by those who should know better—that they must accept a purely logical process, operating on the basis of sense-presented objects alone, as the natural movement of the mind in its discovery of God, and that any sort of Anselmian "monstration" is inadmissible.

I may illustrate a common attitude by a few incidents in my own experience. A friend of mine, a priest, once called on me with a request for a cast-iron proof that we have immortal souls. He had been talking to 'bus-drivers about their souls, and they had shown a marked lack of interest in the subject or even

*An excerpt from *The Basis of Belief* by Illtyd Trethowan. New York: Hawthorn Books, 1961. pp. 127-130.

a general scepticism in regard to it. I had to say that I thought there was no such argument (the proof from the immateriality of the soul being inconclusive), and that in practice belief in the immortality of the soul followed on belief in God, not the other way around. My friend then asked for the knock-down proof of God's existence. He had carried away from his ecclesiastical studies the conviction that rational argument was the sheet-anchor of Catholic apologetics; it had never been quite clear to him how it worked out in the matter of God's existence, but he had no doubt that it was just a question of making the right moves. What were they? Again I had to say that there were, in my opinion, no right moves of the sort which he obviously wanted, no succession of simple statements guaranteed to produce God's existence as their conclusion on pain of a logical contradiction. I then tried to explain how, in my opinion, one should proceed in the matter and ended by suggesting that the 'bus-drivers might be persuaded to read St. John's Gospel and perhaps his Epistles (this was no doubt an over-optimistic suggestion; it is not easy to imagine a 'bus-driver reading St. John, even in Pelican form, while he is off duty at the depot or while the rest of the family watch television). My friend was horrified. He went off in a mood of deep depression, not concealing his suspicions of my orthodoxy and muttering about the Vatican Council and the impropriety of relying in any way on "religious experience."

What happens at the receiving end when the method of "knock-down" argument is attempted could be illustrated at great length. The other day a seventeen-year-old, in an essay for me, had occasion to remark that someone had once tried to prove God's existence to him by using the principle of causality. The argument, he said, was a "flop." If it claims to be fool-proof, it always is. For until we begin to talk about a cause of being, we are saying nothing to the purpose, and as soon as we begin to talk of it we are talking about God. And there is no smooth transition, no logical bridge, from the one sort of talk to the other. It was, I think, attempting a proof for intelligent sixth-formers in the 'thirties which first brought this home to me. It is natural enough to assume at first that the abstract principle of causality is a philosophical truth which anybody can see if he has a mind to, and that one's conviction that God exists is based upon it.[7] You try to put the argument in a simple

7. On attempts to prove God's existence by means of abstract principles some valuable remarks will be found in the last chapter of *The Principle of Sufficient Reason in Some Scholastic Systems*, by Fr. E.G. Gurr, S.J. (Marquette University Press, 1959).

convincing form. Things change, and this means that there is a movement from a previous state of a thing to a latter state. The world has been changing from one state to another for millions of years. But there must be something about it which was always there—otherwise there would be nothing in the long run for the changes to be changes *from*. And how could the original state of the world (gases and what not) produce beasts and men? "But, sir, why shouldn't one stage change into another so that what you have left is quite different from what you started with? Like a sock that gets mended and mended until there is nothing of the *sock* left at all? And why shouldn't this have been going on for *ever?*" At this point there is nothing to fall back on except the assertion: "Anyway, nothing will come of nothing—there *must* be a source of being." "But why, sir? How can you *prove* it?"

Nothing will come of nothing, indeed, but this must be *seen*. And I found myself realizing that I had not myself become a theist as the result of any strictly logical process. In a vague way I had always been a theist, or at least I had had a "notion" of God which had eventually become more than just a "notion" —a conviction. The more I thought about it, the more obvious it became that although the "notion" had arisen in connection with ordinary experience (and was made more plausible by a number of commonsense arguments) it could not be laid out in a solid chain of reasonings. And the ordinary experience with which it was connected proved to be the experience of the moral or, if you will, of the spiritual life rather than the experience of external phenomena. When I said to myself, "There must be a cause, a universal cause," I was simply registering the fact that my "notion" had turned into a conviction. I had simply seen that there *is* a universal cause; I had apprehended it in its operations.

Doubtless it is unwise to begin a discussion by informing someone that he has a knowledge of God, although he may not think so. We should rather suggest to him that his own experience contains some hint of God's existence, although he may not have recognized it for what it is. We should then offer him reasons for supposing that this is the case, and a good deal has been said on those lines in the present book. There is no question, then, of denying the necessity of rational processes or of appealing to an experience unsupported by reason. The point is that the reasoning must provoke the experience, but that it cannot of itself *produce* the experience or substitute for it. It is a question of leading people, by considering the workings of reason, to consider what reason is in itself, what the *mind* is. It is not necessary to use such expressions as "apprehension," "awareness of God" and so forth; it is often better not to do so. The philosopher, who wants to have a coherent and articulated account of what is going on, must use these words. Others may find it more helpful to think in terms of desire or obligation; they may be led to "apprehend" more easily if they do so.[8] There is no objection, then, to a rational dialectic which does not make undue claims and which proceeds in a tentative and human manner, not like a steamroller.

---

8. Even so they will probably not use the language of "knowledge" because the knowledge of God is so different from other knowledge. And in any case they may continue to suppose that, in view of its obscurity, it cannot be in any way direct.

DYNAMICS OF FAITH*
By Paul Tillich

Paul Tillich, one of America's most noted Protestant theologians, believes that there is hardly a word in the religious language which is more subject to misunderstandings, distortions and questionable definitions than the word "faith." He states the term "faith" is currently more conducive of disease than of health: "It confuses, misleads, creates alternately skepticism and fanaticism, intellectual resistance and emotional surrender." The following selection analyzes faith as ultimate concern and contrasts faith and doubt.

WHAT FAITH IS

Faith as Ultimate Concern

Faith is the state of being ultimately concerned: the dynamics of faith are the dynamics of man's ultimate concern. Man, like every living being, is concerned about many things, above all about those which condition his very existence, such as food and shelter. But man, in contrast to other living beings, has spiritual concerns—cognitive, aesthetic, social, political. Some of them are urgent, often extremely urgent, and each of them as well as the vital concerns can claim ultimacy for a human life or the life of a social group. If it claims ultimacy it demands the total surrender of him who accepts this claim, and it promises total fulfillment even if all other claims have to be subjected to it or rejected in its name. If a national group makes the life and growth of the nation its ultimate concern, it demands that all other concerns, economic well-being, health and life, family, aesthetic and cognitive truth, justice and humanity, be sacrificed. The extreme nationalisms of our century are laboratories for the study of what ultimate concern means in all aspects of human existence, including the smallest concern of one's daily life. Everything is centered in the only god, the nation—a god who certainly proves to be a demon, but who shows clearly the unconditional character of an ultimate concern.

---

*From pp. 1-4, 16-22 in *Dynamics of Faith* by Paul Tillich, Volume 10 of *World Perspectives*. Planned and Edited by Ruth Nanda Anshen. Copyright © 1957 by Paul Tillich. By permission of Harper and Row, Publishers, Inc.

But it is not only the unconditional demand made by that which is one's ultimate concern, it is also the promise of ultimate fulfillment which is accepted in the act of faith. The content of this promise is not necessarily defined. It can be expressed in indefinite symbols or in concrete symbols which cannot be taken literally, like the "greatness" of one's nation in which one participates even if one has died for it, or the conquest of mankind by the "saving race," etc. In each of these cases it is "ultimate fulfillment" that is promised, and it is exclusion from such fulfillment which is threatened if the unconditional demand is not obeyed.

An example—and more than an example—is the faith manifest in the religion of the Old Testament. It also has the character of ultimate concern in demand, threat and promise. The content of this concern is not the nation—although Jewish nationalism has sometimes tried to distort it into that—but the content is the God of justice, who, because he represents justice for everybody and every nation, is called the universal God, the God of the universe. He is the ultimate concern of every pious Jew, and therefore in his name the great commandment is given: "You shall love the Lord your God with all your heart, and with all your soul, and with all your might" (Deut. 6:5). This is what ultimate concern means and from these words the term "ultimate concern" is derived. They state unambiguously the character of genuine faith, the demand of total surrender to the subject of ultimate concern. The Old Testament is full of commands which make the nature of this surrender concrete, and it is full of promises and threats in relation to it. Here also are the promises of symbolic indefiniteness, although they center around fulfillment of the national and individual life, and the threat is the exclusion from such fulfillment through national extinction and individual catastrophe. Faith, for the men of the Old Testament, is the state of being ultimately and unconditionally concerned about Jahweh and about what he represents in demand, threat and promise.

Another example—almost a counter-example, yet nevertheless equally revealing—is the ultimate concern with "success" and with social standing and economic power. It is the god of many people in the highly competitive Western culture and it does what every ultimate concern must do: it demands unconditional surrender to its laws even if the price is the sacrifice of genuine human relations, personal conviction, and creative *eros*. Its threat is social and economic defeat, and its promise—indefinite as all such promises—the fulfillment of one's being. It is the breakdown of this kind of faith which characterizes and makes religiously important most contemporary literature. Not false calculations but a misplaced faith is revealed in novels like *Point of No Return*. When fulfilled, the promise of this faith proves to be empty.

Faith is the state of being ultimately concerned. The content matters infinitely for the life of the believer, but it does not matter for the formal definition of faith. And this is the first step we have to make in order to understand the dynamics of faith.

Faith and Doubt

We now return to a fuller description of faith as an act of the human personality, as its centered and total act. An act of faith is an act of a finite being who is grasped by and turned to the infinite. It is a finite act with all the limitations of a finite act, and it is an act in which the infinite participates beyond the limitations of a finite act. Faith is certain in so far as it is an experience of the holy. But faith is uncertain in so far as the infinite to which it is related is received by a finite being. This element of uncertainty in faith cannot be removed, it must be accepted. And the element in faith which accepts this is courage. Faith includes an element of immediate awareness which gives certainty and an element of uncertainty. To accept this is courage. In the courageous standing of uncertainty, faith shows most visibly its dynamic character.

If we try to describe the relation of faith and courage, we must use a larger concept of courage than that which is ordinarily used.[9] Courage as an element of faith is the daring self-affirmation of one's own being in spite of the powers of "nonbeing" which are the heritage of everything finite. When there is daring and courage there is the possibility of failure. And in every act of faith this possibility is present. The risk must be taken. Whoever makes his nation his ultimate concern needs courage in order to maintain this concern. Only certain is the ultimacy as ultimacy, the infinite passion as infinite passion. This is a reality given to the self with his own nature. It is as immediate and as much beyond doubt as the self is to

9. Cf. Paul Tillich, *The Courage to Be.* Yale University Press.

11

the self. It *is* the self in its self-transcending quality. But there is not certainty of this kind about the content of our ultimate concern, be it nation, success, a god, or the God of the Bible: They all are contents without immediate awareness. Their acceptance as matters of ultimate concern is a risk and therefore an act of courage. There is a risk if what was considered as a matter of ultimate concern proves to be a matter of preliminary and transitory concern—as, for example, the nation. The risk to faith in one's ultimate concern is indeed the greatest risk man can run. For if it proves to be a failure, the meaning of one's life breaks down; one surrenders oneself, including truth and justice, to something which is not worth it. One has given away one's personal center without having a chance to regain it. The reaction of despair in people who have experienced the breakdown of their national claims is an irrefutable proof of the idolatrous character of their national concern. In the long run this is the inescapable result of an ultimate concern, the subject matter of which is not ultimate. And this is the risk faith must take; this is the risk which is unavoidable if a finite being affirms itself. Ultimate concern is ultimate risk and ultimate courage. It is not risk and needs no courage with respect to ultimacy itself. But it is risk and demands courage if it affirms a concrete concern. And every faith has a concrete element in itself. It is concerned about something or somebody. But this something or this somebody may prove to be not ultimate at all. Then faith is a failure in its concrete expression, although it is not a failure in the experience of the unconditional itself. A god disappears; divinity remains. Faith risks the vanishing of the concrete god in whom it believes. It may well be that with the vanishing of the god the believer breaks down without being able to re-establish his centered self by a new content of his ultimate concern. This risk cannot be taken away from any act of faith. There is only one point which is a matter not of risk but of immediate certainty and herein lies the greatness and the pain of being human; namely, one's standing between one's finitude and one's potential infinity.

All this is sharply expressed in the relation of faith and doubt. If faith is understood as belief that something is true, doubt is incompatible with the act of faith. If faith is understood as being ultimately concerned, doubt is a necessary element in it. It is a consequence of the risk of faith.

The doubt which is implicit in faith is not a doubt about facts or conclusions. It is not the same doubt which is the lifeblood of scientific research. Even the most orthodox theologian does not deny the right of methodological doubt in matters of empirical inquiry or logical deduction. A scientist who would say that a scientific theory is beyond doubt would at that moment cease to be scientific. He may believe that the theory can be trusted for all practical purposes. Without such belief no technical application of a theory would be possible. One could attribute to this kind of belief pragmatic certainty sufficient for action. Doubt in this case points to the preliminary character of the underlying theory.

There is another kind of doubt, which we could call skeptical in contrast to the scientific doubt which we could call methodological. The skeptical doubt is an attitude toward all the beliefs of man, from sense experiences to religious creeds. It is more an attitude than an assertion. For as an assertion it would conflict with itself. Even the assertion that there is no possible truth for man would be judged by the skeptical principle and could not stand as an assertion. Genuine skeptical doubt does not use the form of an assertion. It is an attitude of actually rejecting any certainty. Therefore, it cannot be refuted logically. It does not transform its attitude into a proposition. Such an attitude necessarily leads either to despair or cynicism, or to both alternately. And often, if this alternative becomes intolerable, it leads to indifference and the attempt to develop an attitude of complete unconcern. But since man is that being who is essentially concerned about his being, such an escape finally breaks down. This is the dynamics of skeptical doubt. It has an awakening and liberating function, but it also can prevent the development of a centered personality. For personality is not possible without faith. The despair about truth by the skeptic shows that truth is still his infinite passion. The cynical superiority over every concrete truth shows that truth is still taken seriously and that the impact of the question of an ultimate concern is strongly felt. The skeptic, so long as he is a serious skeptic, is not without faith, even though it has no concrete content.

The doubt which is implicit in every act of faith is neither the methodological nor the skeptical doubt. It is the doubt which accompanies every risk. It is not the permanent doubt of the scientist, and it is not the transitory doubt of the skeptic, but it is the doubt of him who is ultimately concerned about a concrete content. One could call it the existential doubt, in contrast to the methodological and the skeptical doubt. It does not question whether a special proposition is true or false. It does not reject every concrete truth, but it is aware of the element of insecurity in every existential truth. At the same time, the doubt which is implied in faith accepts this insecurity and takes it into itself in an act of courage. Faith includes courage. Therefore, it can include the doubt about itself. Certainly faith and courage are not identical. Faith has other elements besides courage and courage has other functions beyond affirming faith. Nevertheless, an act in which courage accepts risk belongs to the dynamics of faith.

This dynamic concept of faith seems to give no place to that restful affirmative confidence which we find in the documents of all great religions, including Christianity. But this is not the case. The dynamic concept of faith is the result of a conceptual analysis, both of the subjective and of the objective side of faith. It is by no means the description of an always actualized state of the mind. An analysis of structure is not the description of a state of things. The confusion of these two is a source of many misunderstandings and errors in all realms of life. An example, taken from the current discussion of anxiety, is typical of this confusion. The description of anxiety as the awareness of one's finitude is sometimes criticized as untrue from the point of view of the ordinary state of mind. Anxiety, one says, appears under special conditions but is not an ever-present implication of man's finitude. Certainly anxiety as an acute experience appears under definite conditions. But the underlying structure of finite life is the universal condition which makes the appearance of anxiety under special conditions possible. In the same way doubt is not a permanent experience within the act of faith. But it is always present as an element in the structure of faith. This is the difference between faith and immediate evidence either of perceptual or of logical character. There is no faith without an intrinsic "in spite of" and the courageous affirmation of oneself in the state of ultimate concern. This intrinsic element of doubt breaks into the open under special individual and social conditions. If doubt appears, it should not be considered as the negation of faith, but as an element which was always and will always be present in the act of faith. Existential doubt and faith are poles of the same reality, the state of ultimate concern.

The insight into this structure of faith and doubt is of tremendous practical importance. Many Christians, as well as members of other religious groups, feel anxiety, guilt and despair about what they call "loss of faith." But serious doubt is confirmation of faith. It indicates the seriousness of the concern, its unconditional character. This also refers to those who as future or present ministers of a church experience not only scientific doubt about doctrinal statements—this is as necessary and perpetual as theology is a perpetual need—but also existential doubt about the message of their church, e.g., that Jesus can be called the Christ. The criterion according to which they should judge themselves is the seriousness and ultimacy of their concern about the content of both their faith and their doubt.

GABRIEL MARCEL*
By Seymour Cain

Gabriel Marcel, a twentieth century existentialist philosopher, explains his meaning of prayer and the life of prayer. He believes all meaningful relations both human and divine are personal I-Thou relationships. He says: "All relation of being to being is personal . . . all spiritual life is essentially a dialogue." This I-Thou relation is entirely different from the posture of otherness as an "it." The danger of all prayer as well as in human relations is turning them into "its." Buber believes that only as the other is truly thou for me, do I truly become I for myself, for the thou discovers me to myself. I am truly I only over against a thou for whom I also am a thou. The human I-Thou anticipates the divine I-Thou, mystic union experience.

GABRIEL MARCEL

Prayer is for Marcel the prime example of the relation to the Absolute *Thou,* of invocation and mutuality. Prayer is not a pragmatic technique, a means of securing our finite ends through the absolute recourse. "In this sense, pragmatism is the negation of all religion."[10] Prayer is a matter of being, and of being-with, not of having. "I can pray to be more, not to have more."[11] Prayer can transform my *being,* but it can add nothing to my *having*—to my finite possessions, "inner" or "outer." It transcends that banal distinction, for it is not a matter of mere subjective "states of soul" as against "material things." It is a matter of being and being-with, of a *we*-community, directed toward the absolute being who is always *thou* and never *it* for us. In this view, intercessory prayer is not only possible, it is necessarily implied. But I cannot pray for another person insofar as he is *it* for me, for his use-value ("O God, I pray Thee to make my servant well so I can receive guests this weekend!"). I can only pray for him, as he is *thou* for me, a real being and self, as *we are* in a spiritual community, as

---

*Reprinted with permission from *Gabriel Marcel* by Seymour Cain. Atlantic Highlands, New Jersey: Humanities Press, 1963, pp. 41-46.

10. *Journal metaphysique,* p. 258 (English trans., p. 266).
11. *Ibid.,* p. 219 (English trans., p. 224).

we are we. "There is, at the base of prayer, a will to union with my brothers, without which it would be deprived of all religious value."[12]

Prayer, for Marcel, implies something like the traditional omnicompetence of the divine will expressed in the Biblical phrase, "For God all things are possible." It implies that the world is not set up in a permanent order, a course that runs in pre-established grooves, which the ultimate will cannot change. "To pray is to refuse to admit that all is given; it is to invoke reality treated as will.[13] Prayer has to do with the immediate present, the moment, the once-for-all, the unique now and new. Prayer is renewal, the "active negation of experience," the opposite of passive conformity to the customary way of things. The religious soul rerecognizes no precedents, no established, unquestionable, acquired order. It does recognize an absolute will that transcends all establishments and precedents, that can break in and will uniquely and anew. And it avows an utter dependence on this will, the will of the Absolute *Thou* that wills the person who prays in his incomparable uniqueness, and hence that wills all the things and events of the world in their incomparable uniqueness. The utter dependence implied in prayer is not a matter of surrender to overwhelming external force or a fatalistic acceptance of an inevitable abstract order. It is a free and spontaneous affirmation within a mutual *I-thou* relation—"*Thy* will be done"—not conformity with an impersonal law or order. Above all, it is not a passive surrender to divine "predestination," which in its commonly understood sense is, for Marcel, a contradiction in terms, for nothing can be absolutely pre-established and inevitable for God. "If I abandon myself entirely to God, it is not to Him that I abandon myself."[14] One of Marcel's plays, *Grace,* includes eloquent warnings against the "temptation" of the "abyss" of predestination.[15]

Like any *I-thou* relation, prayer is not verifiable from the outside, by a detached third party. It is also not verifiable as to its "efficacy" by the person who prays. Marcel insists that the divine response cannot be tested by definite criteria or treated

---

12. *Journal metaphysique,* p. 258 (English trans., p. 265).
13. *Ibid.,* p. 219 (English trans., p. 224).
14. *Journal metaphysique,* p. 259.
15. Pere Andre warns Gerard: "Beware of the abyss that awaits the predestined" *(Le Seuil Invisible,* p. 107).

as a casual process. Given the assumed relation, no such question can possibly occur. My prayer is always addressed to that infinite being who is the Absolute *Thou* for me, who cannot fail to hear and understand and respond to my prayer. In this sense, no truly addressed prayer can fail to be efficacious, though not always in an obvious way. Once I inquire about God's attitude and response toward my prayer, I step outside of the *I-thou* relation and transform my prayer into an object, into a not-prayer.

This may seem a circular argument, in which the *I-thou* relation, as immediate experience, is its own proof. In a sense, this is true and has to be so. But prayer involves being-with and a transformation of being, according to Marcel. The sense of the presence of the Absolute *Thou* must be there, and so must the genuine "invocation" by the human person, who enters into and opens himself to the relation. Also there must be some sense of transformation, of real change, of an aid that entirely transcends the kind of aid I can get from other human beings. And although he rules out the attainment of finite goods from the scope of prayer, Marcel is clear that we can pray for the sick and the missing, and for miracles, without, however, *testing* the absolute power we pray to by objective observation and checks.

Another significant instance of the ultimate *I-thou* relation is the experience of suffering, evil, frustration, and contradiction. The religious man sees this experience as a "trial" or "test" that is "sent" from a transcendent realm. Such an understanding is possible only within the personal relation to the Absolute *Thou* (as between Job and God). Trial is not a matter of objective causality, with God as an external agent acting on man as his object, understood retrospectively as a past cause producing a present result. "To think religiously is to think the present under the aspect of divine will"[16]—that is, of the Absolute *Thou, Thy* will. The attitude of the religious man (of the Psalmist, for instance)—in the present moment, in immediate experience—is that "I [my life and its trials] am willed *by Thee*."

Again, this attitude is not fatalistic, a surrender to the mere determining power of an omnipotent being who is without care or love. For "trial" may be saving as well as overwhelming. It menaces my being, my integral wholeness, and my faith—

16. *Journal metaphysique,* p. 229 (English trans., p. 235).

defined as the "power of adherence to being." It involves temptation—to succumb to the "menace" of spiritual annihilation and lostness, of meaninglessness and nihilism, in the face of sorrow and disillusion. But it also involves the possibility of the conservation and transformation of the menaced being, through a self-judgment or self-relation which results in a rediscovery and reunification of the self. "Trial," with its menace and temptation, forces me to measure myself, to find my own height or depth in urgent action. This happy ending is not a guaranteed result, for trial is not a sure thing; it involves a spiritual "wager." It is not mere play-acting, a predetermined charade, but the real thing, where my soul and very being are "at stake."

This peril of the soul or being is characteristic of human existence, of the whole of life, and begins as soon as I come into existence. Life itself is a trial, testing my being and my adherence to being, my self-maintenance and my relation to ultimate, transcendent reality. The world is so constituted that my soul and my being must be constantly subjected to the corrosive dissolvents of experience and criticism. "To be, means to withstand this test, this progressive dissolution. To deny being would be to claim that nothing can withstand the test."[17] This possibility is the basis both of pessimism and nihilism—which Marcel grants are theoretically legitimate— and of religious existence. "There is religious life only for souls which know themselves menaced," and who, in this critical situation, this unique "condition of the heart," pray that the "stake" be saved.[18] Indeed, the soul, ontologically understood, comes really to be "only on condition of having been saved," on the other side of the "dialectic of experience," of "the trial of life." Trial involves "an act that attains being," and the triumphant endurance and emergence of the innermost, vital, dynamic, active core of the self.[19]

17. *Journal metaphysique,* p. 178 (English trans., p. 180).
18. *Ibid.,* p. 260 (English trans., p. 268).
19. *Journal metaphysique,* pp. 282, 179 f. (English trans., pp. 291, 181 f.).

THE MIND'S ROAD TO GOD*
St. Bonaventure

Bonaventure, a native of Tuscany, was born Giovanni di Fidanza in 1221. He entered the Franciscan order and in the short space of fifteen years rose to be seventh general of that order. Professor of theology at the University of Paris, Bishop of Albano, and created a cardinal before his death in 1274, he was widely respected in his life and is mentioned as a saint in Dante's Paradiso. *His little book,* The Mind's Road to God, *is a metaphysical masterpiece of Christian spirituality. Notice the role of grace and the response of prayer that he stresses in the development of sanctification.*

THE MENDICANT'S VISION IN THE WILDERNESS
Of the Stages in the Ascent to God and of His Reflection in His Traces in the Universe[20]

Blessed is the man whose help is from Thee. In his heart he hath disposed to ascend by steps, in the vale of tears, in the place which he hath set [Ps., 83, 6]. Since beatitude is nothing else than the fruition of the highest good, and the highest good is above us, none can be made blessed unless he ascend above himself, not by the ascent of his body but by that of his heart. But we cannot be raised above ourselves except by a higher power raising us up. For howsoever the interior steps are disposed, nothing is accomplished unless it is accompanied by divine aid. Divine help, however, comes to those who seek it from their hearts humbly and devoutly; and this means to sigh for it in this vale of tears, aided only by fervent prayer. Thus

*From Saint Bonaventure: *The Mind's Road to God,* translated by George Boas,© 1953, by the Liberal Arts Press, Inc., reprinted by permission of The Bobbs-Merrill Company, Inc., pp. 7-10.

20. I have translated the Latin *speculatio,* which appears over and over again in this work, in a variety of ways. St. Bonaventure plays upon its various shades of meaning—*reflection, speculation, consideration*—for he seems haunted by the basic metaphor of the universe's being a sort of mirror *(speculum)* in which God is to be seen. The Italian and French translators have the advantage of those of us who write English, for they have merely to transliterate the Latin word. We have a similar difficulty in the Latin word *vestigia,* which I have translated *traces.* It will hardly do to write *vestiges* or *footprints,* and *traces* is not much better. St. Bonaventure simply means that by considering the work of art one will know the artist. His handiwork shows traces of his workmanship. But we are likely to think of traces as something which are left behind, whereas God is not to be thought of as having created the world and then left it alone, as Pascal said of Descartes' God.

prayer is the mother and source of ascent *(sursum-actionis)* in God. Therefore Dionysius, in his book, *Mystical Theology* [ch. 1, 1], wishing to instruct us in mental elevation, prefaces his work by prayer. Therefore let us pray and say to the Lord our God, "Conduct me, O Lord, in Thy way, and I will walk in Thy truth; let my heart rejoice that it may fear Thy name" [Ps., 85, 11] . . . .

Now at the Creation, man was made fit for the repose of contemplation, and therefore God placed him in a paradise of delight [Gen., 2, 16]. But turning himself away from the true light to mutable goods, he was bent over by his own sin, and the whole human race by original sin, which doubly infected human nature, ignorance infecting man's mind and concupiscence his flesh. Hence man, blinded and bent, sits in the shadows and does not see the light of heaven unless grace with justice succor him from concupiscence, and knowledge with wisdom against ignorance. All of which is done through Jesus Christ, Who of God is made unto us wisdom and justice and sanctification and redemption [I Cor., 1, 30]. He is the virtue and wisdom of God, the Word incarnate, the author of grace and truth—that is, He has infused the grace of charity, which, since it is from a pure heart and good conscience and unfeigned faith, rectifies the whole soul . . .

Therefore he who wishes to ascend to God must, avoiding sin, which deforms nature, exercise the above-mentioned natural powers for regenerating grace, and do this through prayer. He must strive toward purifying justice, and this in intercourse; toward the illumination of knowledge, and this in meditation; toward the perfection of wisdom, and this in contemplation. Now just as no one comes to wisdom save through grace, justice, and knowledge, so none comes to contemplation save through penetrating meditation, holy conversation, and devout prayer. Just as grace is the foundation of the will's rectitude and of the enlightenment of clear and penetrating reason, so, first, we must pray; secondly, we must live holily; thirdly, we must strive toward the reflection of truth and, by our striving, mount step by step until we come to the high mountain where we shall see the God of gods in Sion [Ps., 83, 8].

THE COST OF DISCIPLESHIP*
By Dietrich Bonhoeffer

The Cost of Discipleship almost needs no introduction, since it is a modern Christian classic. Bonhoeffer's objective is to criticize those who express belief in Christ without following Him in discipleship. He says: "Cheap grace is the grace we bestow on ourselves . . . the preaching of forgiveness without requiring repentance, baptism without church discipline, communion without confession. Cheap grace is grace without discipleship . . . Costly grace is the gospel which must be sought again and again, the gift which must be asked for, the door at which a man must knock . . . It is costly because it costs a man his life, and it is grace because it gives a man the only true life."

THE COST OF DISCIPLESHIP

If we would follow Jesus we must take certain definite steps. The first step, which follows the call, cuts the disciple off from his previous existence. The call to follow at once produces a new situation. To stay in the old situation makes discipleship impossible. Levi must leave the receipt of custom and Peter his nets in order to follow Jesus. One would have thought that nothing so drastic was necessary at such an early stage. Could not Jesus have initiated the publican into some new religious experience, and leave them as they were before? He could have done so, had he not been the incarnate Son of God. But since he is the Christ, he must make it clear from the start that his word is not an abstract doctrine, but the re-creation of the whole life of man. The only right and proper way is quite literally to go with Jesus. The call to follow implies that there is only one way of believing on Jesus Christ, and that is by leaving all and going with the incarnate Son of God.

The first step places the disciple in the situation where faith is possible. If he refuses to follow and stays behind, he does not learn how to believe. He who is called must go out of his situation in which he cannot believe, into the situation in which, first and foremost, faith is possible. But this step is not the first stage of a career. Its sole justification is that it brings the disciple into fellowship with Jesus which will be victorious.

*Reprinted with permission from *The Cost of Discipleship* by Dietrich Bonhoeffer. New York: Macmillan, 1972, pp. 67-71.

So long as Levi sits at the receipt of custom, and Peter at his nets, they could both pursue their trade honestly and dutifully, and they might both enjoy religious experiences, old and new. But if they want to believe in God, the only way is to follow his incarnate Son.

Until that day, everything had been different. They could remain in obscurity, pursuing their work as the quiet in the land, observing the law and waiting for the coming of the Messiah. But now he has come, and his call goes forth. Faith can no longer mean sitting still and waiting—they must rise and follow him. The call frees them from all earthly ties, and binds them to Jesus Christ alone. They must burn their boats and plunge into absolute insecurity in order to learn the demand and the gift of Christ. Had Levi stayed at his post, Jesus might have been his present help in trouble, but not the Lord of his whole life. In other words Levi would never have learnt to believe. The new situation must be created, in which it is possible to believe on Jesus as God incarnate; that is the impossible situation in which everything is staked solely on the word of Jesus. Peter had to leave the ship and risk his life on the sea, in order to learn both his own weakness and the almightly power of his Lord. If Peter had not taken the risk, he would never have learnt the meaning of faith. Before he can believe, the utterly impossible and ethically irresponsible situation on the waves of the sea must be displayed. The road to faith passes through obedience to the call of Jesus. Unless a definite step is demanded, the call vanishes into thin air, and if men imagine that they can follow Jesus without taking this step. they are deluding themselves like fanatics.

It is an extremely hazardous procedure to distinguish between a situation where faith is possible and one where it is not. We must first realize that there is nothing in the situation to tell us to which category it belongs. It is only the call of Jesus which makes it a situation where faith is possible. Secondly, a situation where faith is possible can never be demonstrated from the human side. Discipleship is not an offer man makes to Christ. It is only the call which creates the situation. Thirdly, this situation never possesses any intrinsic worth or merit of its own. It is only through the call that it receives its justification. Last, but not least, the situation in which faith is possible is itself only rendered possible through faith.

The idea of a situation in which faith is possible is only a way of stating the facts of a case in which the following two propositions hold good and are equally true: *only he who believes is obedient, and only he who is obedient believes.*

It is quite unbiblical to hold the first proposition without the second. We think we understand when we hear that obedience is possible only where there is faith. Does not obedience follow faith as good fruit grows on a good tree? First, faith, then obedience. If by that we mean that it is faith which justifies, and not the act of obedience, all well and good, for that is the essential and unexceptionable presupposition of all that follows. If, however, we make a chronological distinction between faith and obedience, and make obedience subsequent to faith, we are divorcing the one from the other—and then we get the practical question, when must obedience begin? Obedience remains separated from faith. From the point of view of justification it is necessary thus to separate them, but we must never lose sight of their essential unity. For faith is only real when there is obedience, never without it, and faith only becomes faith in the act of obedience.

Since, then, we cannot adequately speak of obedience as the consequence of faith, and since we must never forget the indissoluble unity of the two, we must place the one proposition that only he who believes is obedient alongside the other, that only he who is obedient believes. In the one case faith is the condition of obedience, and in the other obedience the condition of faith. In exactly the same way in which obedience is called the consequence of faith, it must also be called the presupposition of faith.

Only the obedient believe. If we are to believe, we must obey a concrete command. Without this preliminary step of obedience, our faith will only be pious humbug, and lead us to the grace which is not costly. Everything depends on the first step. It has a unique quality of its own. The first step of obedience makes Peter leave his nets, and later get out of the ship; it calls upon the young man to leave his riches. Only this new existence, created through obedience, can make faith possible.

This first step must be regarded to start with as an external work, which effects the change from one existence to another. It is a step within everybody's capacity, for it lies within the limits of human freedom. It is an act within the sphere of the natural law *(justitia civilis)* and in that sphere man is free. Although Peter cannot achieve his own conversion, he can leave his nets. In the gospels the very first step man must take is an act which radically affects his whole existence. The Roman Catholic Church demanded this step as an extraordinary possibility which only monks could achieve, while the rest of the faithful must content themselves with an unconditional submission to the Church and its ordinances. The Lutheran confessions also significantly recognize the first step. Having dealt effectively with the danger of Pelagianism, they find it both possible and necessary to leave room for the first external act which is the essential preliminary to faith. This step there takes the form of an invitation to come to the Church where the word of salvation is proclaimed. To take this step it is not necessary to surrender one's freedom. Come to church! You can do that of your own free will. You can leave your home on a Sunday morning and come to hear the sermon. If you will not, you are of your own free will excluding yourself from the place where faith is a possibility. Thus the Lutheran confessions show their awareness of a situation where faith is a possibility, and of a situation where it is not. Admittedly they tend to soft-pedal it as though they were almost ashamed of it. But there it is, and it shows that they are just as aware as the gospels of the importance of the first external step.

THE SCALE OF PERFECTION*
By Walter Hilton

There is very little known of Walter Hilton himself, except that he was a Canon Regular of St. Augustine at the Priory of St. Peter at Thurgarten, near Southwell, England. He died at the Priory probably in 1395. The Scale of Perfection *is surely one of the great spiritual classics of the Renaissance era. The English spiritual writers were noted for their practical advice in the spiritual journey. Indeed, Hilton explains the whole spiritual adventure with much practical insight. Notice how he separates reformed in faith (salvation) from reformed in faith and feeling (sanctification). Probably no English devotional work has had so wide and enduring an influence as* The Scale of Perfection.

THE SCALE OF PERFECTION
*How those who love this world hinder the reformation of their souls in various ways***

But certain of these people say: 'I would gladly love God, be good, and renounce love of the world if I could, but I have not the grace to do so. If I had the same grace as a good man I would live as he does; but since I have not this grace, I cannot do it.' I reply that it is quite true that they have no grace, and therefore remain in their sin and cannot escape it. But this will not help them, nor does it excuse them before God, because it is their own fault. They hinder themselves so greatly and in so many ways that the light of grace cannot shine in them nor dwell in their hearts. Some of them are so obstinate that they do not desire grace or a good life, for they realize that if this were the case they would have to give up their love and desire for worldly things. And they do not wish to do this, because these things are so pleasant to them that they do not wish to forgo them. They would furthermore have to undertake works of penance, such as fasting, keeping vigils, praying and other practices which discipline the body and subdue its sinful inclinations. And they cannot do this because it appears so

---

*Reprinted from *The Scale of Perfection* by Walter Hilton,© Geoffrey Chapman Publishers, 1975, with the permission of Abbey Press, St. Meinrad, Indiana, pp. 61-61 and 71-74.

**This excerpt is from Number 23, Chapter 15.

painful and unpleasant to them that they are frightened to think of it. As a result these cowardly and unhappy people continue in their sins.

Some would seem to desire grace, and begin to prepare themselves for it. But their wills are extraordinarily weak, for they immediately yield to any temptation that arises, although it is clearly contrary to the laws of God. They are so accustomed to giving way that resistance to sin seems impossible to them, and this imaginary difficulty gradually saps their will-power and destroys it.

Some, again, feel the influence of grace when their conscience pricks them for their evil life and prompts them to abandon it. But this suggestion is so painful and displeasing that they refuse to entertain it. They run away and forget it if they can, seeking outward distraction in creatives so as not to feel this inward pricking of conscience [. . .]

Those who love this world are advised what to do if their souls are to be reformed before they die

Although such people are fully aware that they are not in a state of grace and are in mortal sin, they do not care; they are not sorry, nor do they give the matter a thought. They pass their time in worldly pastimes and pleasures, and the further they are from grace, the more hectic their pursuits. Perhaps some are even glad that they have no grace, so that they may, as it were, feel more free to gratify their desire for worldly pleasures, as though God were asleep and could not see them. This is one of the gravest errors, for by their perverseness they prevent the light of grace entering their souls. For the light of grace shines on all spiritual beings, ready to enter where it is welcomed, just as the sun shines on all material things wherever it is not prevented. Thus St. John says in the Gospel: *Lux in tenebris lucet, et tenebrae non comprehenderunt* (John 1:5). The light of grace shines in the darkness—that is, on the hearts of men darkened by sin—but the darkness does not welcome it. In other words, these blind hearts do not receive this light of grace or profit by it. Just as a blind man is bathed in sunlight when he stands in it, but cannot see it or walk by it, similarly a soul blinded by mortal sin is bathed in this light of grace, but is none the better for it, because he is blind and does not or will not realize his blindness. The greatest obstacle to grace is a person's refusal to admit his own blindness because of pride; or if he does realize it, he ignores it and continues to enjoy himself as though all were well with him.

I urge all who are blinded and enslaved by the love of the world in this way, and those in whom the true beauty of human nature is distorted, to consider their souls and prepare them to receive grace as well as they can [. . .] And if they did so, grace would be given them. It would drive away all darkness and hardness of heart, and all weakness of will; it would give them strength to abandon the false love of the world where it leads to mortal sin. For there is no soul in this life so estranged from God by a perverse following of mortal sin that it cannot be corrected and restored by grace to purity of living if only it will humbly surrender its will to God, amend its ways, and sincerely ask his grace and forgiveness. It must accept full responsibility for its own guilty state, and not try to blame God. For Holy Scripture says: *Nolo mortem peccatoris, sed magis ut convertatur et vivat* (Ezek. 33:11). God says: I do not desire the death of a sinner, but rather that he should turn to me and live. And it is the will of our Lord that the most obstinate and misguided sinner living should be reformed to his likeness if he will but amend his life and seek for grace.

How reform of feeling and faith cannot be achieved all at once; it is effected by grace after a long time and with much bodily and spiritual effort

As I said previously, this reformation in faith can be achieved quite easily. Reformation in faith and feeling must follow; this is not so easily attained, and comes only after patient and prolonged effort. For all God's chosen are reformed in faith, although they may still remain in the lowest degree of charity; but reformation in feeling comes only to souls who reach a state of perfection, and it cannot be achieved all at once. A soul can reach it only through great grace and by prolonged spiritual effort, but it must first be healed of its spiritual sickness. Its bitter passions, bodily desires, and unregenerate feelings have to be burned out of the heart by the fire of desire, and new feelings of burning love and spiritual light have to be infused by grace. Then the soul begins to draw near to perfection and reformation in feeling.

The soul's progress is like that of a man who has been brought near to death by bodily illness. Although he may be given medicine which restores him and saves his life, he cannot immediately get up and go to work like a man in full health. His bodily weakness prevents this, so that he has to wait a good while, continue with his medicine, and carefully follow his doctor's instructions until his health is fully restored. Similarly in the spiritual life, although one who has been brought near to spiritual death by mortal sin can be restored to life by the medicine of the sacrament of penance, and saved from damnation, he is not at once healed of all his passions and worldly desires, nor is he capable of contemplation. He must wait a long time and take good care of himself, and he must order his life so as to recover full health of soul. However, if he takes the medicines of a good doctor and uses them regularly and with discretion, he will be restored to spiritual vitality all the sooner, and will attain reformation in feeling.

Reformation in faith is the lowest state of chosen souls, and below this level they cannot well be; but reformation in feeling is the highest state attainable by a soul in this life. But a soul cannot suddenly leap from the lowest to the highest state, any more than a man who wishes to climb a high ladder and sets his foot on the lowest rung can at the next instant fly to the top. He has to mount each rung in succession one after the other until he comes to the highest. So it is in the spiritual life. No one is suddenly endowed with all graces, but when God, the source of all grace, helps and teaches a soul, it can attain this state by sustained spiritual exercises and wisely ordered activity. For without his especial help and inner guidance no soul can reach a state of perfection.

One reason why comparatively few souls achieve reformation in faith and feeling

You may say that since our Lord is so good and gracious, and bestows his gifts so freely, it is surprising that so few souls come to be reformed in feeling, compared with the vast number who do not. It might seem that he is estranged from those who by faith have become his servants, or that he has no regard for them; but this is not true. I think one reason why people are so seldom reformed in feeling is that many who have been reformed in faith do not make a whole-hearted effort to grow in grace, or to lead better lives by means of earnest prayer and meditation, and by other spiritual and bodily exercises. They think it sufficient to avoid mortal sin, and continue to live in the same way. They say that it is enough for them to be saved, and they are content with the lowest place in heaven, wanting nothing higher.

It is possible that some of the elect who lead an active life in the world behave in this way, and this is not altogether surprising, because they are so busy with necessary worldly matters that they cannot devote proper attention to spiritual progress. This is a perilous condition, for they are rising and falling, up and down all day, and never attain any stability in their attempt to lead a good life. However, their way of life affords some kind of excuse. But there are others who have no need to be occupied in worldly business, and who do not have to work very hard to support themselves—for instance, religious people of both sexes who vow themselves to a state of perfection in a religious order, or layfolk who are naturally capable and intelligent. People like these could achieve a high state of grace if they set themselves to do so, and they are all the more culpable if they remain idle and make no attempt to grow in grace, or to attain the love and knowledge of God.

It is most dangerous for a soul that is reformed in faith alone to make no effort to seek God and grow in grace, nor to engage in spiritual activity. It may so easily lose ground already gained, and fall back again into mortal sin. For while the soul remains in the body it cannot stand still; it must either grow in grace or relapse into sin. It behaves like a man drawn up out of a pit, who refuses to leave the edge once he is out. He is certainly a fool, for a little gust of wind or a single incautious movement on his part will send him headlong in a worse condition than before. But if he moves right away from the edge and stands on firm ground he will be much safer, even should a great storm arise. It is similar in the spiritual life with one who has been drawn up out of the pit of sin by reformation in faith. If he thinks himself safe enough once he is no longer in mortal sin, refusing to step away, and staying as close as possible to the brink of hell, he is a fool, for at the smallest temptation of the devil or the flesh he falls into sin again. But if he leaves the pit—that is, if he makes a firm resolve to grow in grace, and makes a real effort to win it by prayer and meditation, and by other good works—then although he may undergo violent temptations, he will not easily relapse into mortal sin.

Since grace is good and brings blessing it amazes me when a person who has so little grace that he could hardly possess less, says: 'I have enough; I need no more.' But although a worldly man may have more possessions than he needs, I never hear one say, 'I have enough; I need no more.' He will always want more and more, and devote his whole mind and resources to obtaining more, because his greed is insatiable. Much more, then, should a chosen soul desire spiritual treasures which last for ever and fill the soul with blessing. The wise soul will never cease to desire grace, however much it may already possess, for whoever desires most will obtain most. Indeed, in so doing it will earn great riches and grow in grace.

INTERIOR CASTLE*
By St. Teresa of Avila

Probably no other books by a Spanish author have received such wide popular acclaim as the Life *and* Interior Castle *of St. Teresa. It is remarkable that a woman who lived in the sixteenth century, who spent most of her life in an enclosed convent, who never had any formal schooling and never aspired to any public fame, should have won such an extraordinary reputation, both among scholars and among the people. Perhaps the two most noted Christian mystics, aside from the Biblical accounts themselves, are St. Teresa and St. John of the Cross. Both were personal friends as well as spiritual giants. Notice the stress Teresa places upon prayer in developing the spiritual life.*

INTERIOR CASTLE
Treats of the beauty and dignity of our souls; makes a comparison by the help of which this may be understood; describes the benefit which comes from understanding it and being aware of the favours which we receive from God; and shows how the door of this castle is prayer.

While I was beseeching Our Lord today that He would speak through me, since I could find nothing to say and had no idea how to begin to carry out the obligation laid upon me by obedience, a thought occurred to me which I will now set down, in order to have some foundation on which to build. I began to think of the soul as if it were a castle made of a single diamond or of very clear crystal, in which there are many rooms,[21] just as in Heaven there are many mansions.[22] Now if we think carefully over this, sisters, the soul of the righteous man is nothing but a paradise, in which, as God tells us, He takes His delight.[23] For what do you think a room will be like which is the

---

*Reprinted from *The Interior Castle* in *The Complete Works of St. Teresa*, trans. and ed. by E. Allison Peers from the critical edition of P. Silverio De Santa Teresa, O.C.D., published in three volumes by Sheed and Ward, Inc., New York. Excerpt from Image Books, 1961, pp. 28-33.

21. [*Aposentos*—a rather more pretentious word than the English "room": dwelling place, abode, apartment.]
22. [*Morados:* derived from *morar,* to dwell, and not, therefore, absolutely identical in sense with "mansions." The reference, however, is to St. John xiv, 2.]
23. Proverbs viii, 31.

delight of a King so mighty, so wise, so pure and so full of all that is good? I can find nothing with which to compare the great beauty of a soul and its great capacity. In fact, however acute our intellects may be, they will no more be able to attain to a comprehension of this than to an understanding of God; for, as He Himself says, He created us in His image and likeness.[24] Now if this is so—and it is—there is no point in our fatiguing ourselves by attempting to comprehend the beauty of this castle; for, though it is His creature, and there is therefore as much difference between it and God as between creature and Creator, the very fact that His Majesty says it is made in His image means that we can hardly form any conception of the soul's great dignity and beauty.[25]

It is no small pity, and should cause us no little shame, that, through our own fault, we do not understand ourselves, or know who we are. Would it not be a sign of great ignorance, my daughters, if a person were asked who he was, and could not say, and had no idea who his father or his mother was, or from what country he came? Though that is great stupidity, our own is incomparably greater if we make no attempt to discover what we are, and only know that we are living in these bodies, and have a vague idea, because we have heard it and because our Faith tells us so, that we possess souls. As to what good qualities there may be in our souls, or Who dwells within them, or how precious they are— those are things which we seldom consider and so we trouble little about carefully preserving the soul's beauty. All our interest is centered in the rough setting of the diamond, and in the outer wall of the castle—that is to say, in these bodies of ours.

Let us now imagine that this castle, as I have said, contains many mansions,[26] some above, others below, others at each side; and in the centre and midst of them all is the chiefest mansion where the most secret things pass between God and the soul. You must think over this comparison very carefully; perhaps God will be pleased to use it to show you something of the favours which He is pleased to grant to souls, and of the differences between them, so far as I have understood this to be possible, for there are so many of them that nobody can possibly understand them all, much less anyone as stupid as I.

24. Genesis i, 26.
25. Here the Saint erased several words and inserted others, leaving the phrase as it is in the text.
26. [*Moradas* (see p. 28, n. 2, above).]

If the Lord grants you these favours, it will be a great consolation to you to know that such things are possible; and, if you never receive any, you can still praise His great goodness. For, as it does us no harm to think of the things laid up for us in Heaven, and of the joys of the blessed, but rather makes us rejoice and strive to attain those joys ourselves, just so it will do us no harm to find that it is possible in this our exile for so great a God to commune with such malodorous worms, and to love Him for His great goodness and boundless mercy. I am sure that anyone who finds it harmful to realize that it is possible for God to grant such favours during this our exile must be greatly lacking in humility and in love of his neighbour; for otherwise how could we help rejoicing that God should grant these favours to one of our brethren when this in no way hinders Him from granting them to ourselves, and that His Majesty should bestow an understanding of His greatness upon anyone soever? Sometimes He will do this only to manifest His power, as He said of the blind man to whom He gave his sight, when the Apostles asked Him if he were suffering for his own sins or for the sins of his parents.[27] He grants these favours, then, not because those who receive them are holier than those who do not, but in order that His greatness may be made known, as we see in the case of Saint Paul and the Magdalen, and in order that we may praise Him in His creatures.

It may be said that these things seem impossible and that it is better not to scandalize the weak. But less harm is done by their disbelieving us than by our failing to edify those to whom God grants these favours, and who will rejoice and will awaken others to a fresh love of Him Who grants such mercies, according to the greatness of His power and majesty. In any case I know that none to whom I am speaking will run into this danger, because they all know and believe that God grants still greater proofs of His love. I am sure that, if any one of you does not believe this, she will never learn it by experience. For God's will is that no bounds should be set to His works. Never do such a thing, then, sisters, if the Lord does not lead you by this road.

Now let us return to our beautiful and delightful castle and see how we can enter it. I seem rather to be talking nonsense; for, if this castle is the soul, there can clearly be no question of our entering it. For we ourselves are the castle: and it would be

27. St. John ix, 2.

absurd to tell someone to enter a room when he was in it already! But you must understand that there are many ways of "being" in a place. Many souls remain in the outer court of the castle, which is the place occupied by the guards; they are not interested in entering it, and have no idea what there is in that wonderful place, or who dwells in it, or even how many rooms it has. You will have read certain books on prayer which advise the soul to enter within itself: and that is exactly what this means.

A short time ago I was told by a very learned man that souls without prayer are like people whose bodies or limbs are paralysed: they possess feet and hands but they cannot control them. In the same way, there are souls so infirm and so accustomed to busying themselves with outside affairs that nothing can be done for them, and it seems as though they are incapable of entering within themselves at all. So accustomed have they grown to living all the time with the reptiles and other creatures to be found in the outer court of the castle that they have almost become like them; and although by nature they are so richly endowed as to have the power of holding converse with none other than God Himself, there is nothing that can be done for them. Unless they strive to realize their miserable condition and to remedy it, they will be turned into pillars of salt for not looking within themselves, just as Lot's wife was because she looked back.[28]

As far as I can understand, the door of entry into this castle is prayer and meditation: I do not say mental prayer rather than vocal, for, if it is prayer at all, it must be accompanied by meditation. If a person does not think Whom he is addressing, and what he is asking for, and who it is that is asking and of Whom he is asking it, I do not consider that he is praying at all even though he be constantly moving his lips. True, it is sometimes possible to pray without paying heed to these things, but that is only because they have been thought about previously; if a man is in the habit of speaking to God's Majesty as he would speak to his slave, and never wonders if he is expressing himself properly, but merely utters the words that come to his lips because he has learned them by heart through constant repetition, I do not call that prayer at all—and God grant no Christian may ever speak to Him so! At any rate, sisters, I hope in God that none of you will, for we are

28. Genesis xix, 26.

accustomed here to talk about interior matters, and that is a good way of keeping oneself from falling into such animal-like habits.[29]

Let us say no more, then, of these paralysed souls, who, unless the Lord Himself comes and commands them to rise, are like the man who had lain beside the pool for thirty years:[30] they are unfortunate creatures and live in great peril. Let us rather think of certain other souls, who do eventually enter the castle. These are very much absorbed in worldly affairs; but their desires are good; sometimes, though infrequently, they commend themselves to Our Lord; and they think about the state of their souls, though not very carefully. Full of a thousand preoccupations as they are, they pray only a few times a month, and as a rule they are thinking all the time of their preoccupations, for they are very much attached to them, and, where their treasure is, there is their heart also.[31] From time to time, however, they shake their minds free of them and it is a great thing that they should know themselves well enough to realize that they are not going the right way to reach the castle door. Eventually they enter the first rooms on the lowest floor, but so many reptiles get in with them that they are unable to appreciate the beauty of the castle or to find any peace within it. Still, they have done a good deal by entering at all.

You will think this is beside the point, daughters, since by the goodness of the Lord you are not one of these. But you must be patient, for there is no other way in which I can explain to you some ideas I have had about certain interior matters concerning prayer. May it please the Lord to enable me to say something about them; for to explain to you what I should like is very difficult unless you have had personal experience; and anyone with such experience, as you will see, cannot help touching upon subjects which, please God, shall, by His mercy, never concern us.

---

29. [*Lit.*, "into such bestiality."] P. Gracian deletes "bestiality" and substitutes "abomination." [I think the translation in the text, however, is a more successful way of expressing what was in St. Teresa's mind: cf. St. John of the Cross's observations on "animal penances"—*penitencias de bestias*—in his *Dark Night*, I, vi *(Complete Works*, I, 365-6).]

30. P. Gracian corrects this to "thirty-eight years." St. John v, 5.

31. St. Matthew vi, 21.

HOLY WISDOM*
By Augustine Baker

Augustine Baker (1575-1641) lived during the unsettling period of Reformation England. His major work Holy Wisdom *created a minor revolution in the approach to spirituality. In his capacity as spiritual advisor to exiled English nuns, he advised flexibility in prayer and meditations rather than a fixed and rigid system that was then in practice. Baker's system was later labeled "Bakerism." Notice the importance Baker gives to a firm resolution as the motivating force in developing sanctification or as he labels it: perfection.*

HOLY WISDOM
Of the necessity of a strong resolution

The end of a contemplative life, therefore, being so supereminently noble and divine that beatified souls do prosecute the same, and no other, in heaven, with this only difference, that the same beatifying object which is now obscurely seen by faith and imperfectly embraced by love shall hereafter be seen clearly and perfectly enjoyed. The primary and most general duty required in souls which by God's vocation do walk in the ways of the spirit, is to admire, love, and long after this union, and to fix an immovable resolution through God's grace and assistance to attempt and persevere in the prosecution of so glorious a design, in despite of all opposition, through light and darkness, through consolations and desolations, etc., as esteeming it to be cheaply purchased, though with the loss of all comforts that nature can find or expect in creatures.

The fixing of such a courageous resolution is of so main importance and necessity that if it should happen to fail or yield to any, though the fiercest temptations, that may occur and are to be expected, so as not to be reassumed, the whole design will be ruined; and therefore devout souls are often-times to renew such a resolution, and especially when any difficulty presents itself; and for that purpose they will oft be put in mind thereof in these following instructions.

It is not to be esteemed loftiness, presumption, or pride to

---

*An excerpt from Augustine Baker: *Holy Wisdom,* translated by Gerard Sitwell, © Ampleforth Abbey; used by permission, Anthony Clarke Books, pp. 17-21.

tend to so sublime an end; but it is a good and laudable ambition, and most acceptable to God; yea, the root of it is true, solid humility joined with the love of God; for it proceeds from a vile esteem and some degrees of a holy hatred of ourselves, from whom we desire to fly; and a just esteem, obedience, and love of God, to whom only we desire to adhere and be inseparably united.

Happy, therefore, is the soul that finds in herself an habitual thirst and longing after this union, if she will seek to assuage it by continual approaches to this Fountain of living waters, labouring thereto with daily external and internal workings. The very tendence to this union, in which our whole essential happiness consists, has in it some degrees of happiness, and is an imperfect union, disposing to a perfect one; for by such internal tendence and aspiring we get by little and little out of nature into God. And that without such an interior tendence and desire no exterior sufferances or observances will imprint any true virtue in the soul, or bring her nearer to God, we see in the example of Suso, who for the first five years of religious profession found no satisfaction in soul at all, notwithstanding all his care and exactness in exterior regular observances and mortifications: he perceived plainly that still he wanted something, but what that was he could not tell, till God was pleased to discover it to him, and put him in the way to attain to his desire, which was in spirit to tend continually to this union, without which all his austerities and observances served little or nothing, as proceeding principally from self-love, self-judgment, and the satisfying of nature even by crossing it.

Let nothing, therefore, deter a well-minded soul from persevering with fervour in this firm resolution. No, not the sight of her daily defects, imperfections, or sins, or remorses for them; but rather let her increase in courage even from her falls, and from the experience of her own impotency let her be incited to run more earnestly and adhere more firmly unto God, by whom she will be enabled to do all things and conquer all resistances.

Now to the end that all sincerity may be used in the delivery of these instructions, and that all vain compliance and flattery may be avoided, the devout soul is to be informed that the way to perfection is (1) both a very long, tedious way; and (2) withal there are to be expected in it many grievous, painful, and bitter temptations and crosses to corrupt nature; as being a way that wholly and universally contradicts and destroys all the vain eases, contentments, interests, and designs of nature, teaching a soul to die unto self-love, self-judgment, and all propriety, and to raise herself out of nature, seeking to live in a region exalted above nature: to wit, the region of the spirit; into which being once come, she will find nothing but light and peace and joy in the Holy Ghost. The which difficulties considered, instead of being discouraged, she will, if she be truly touched with God's Spirit, rather increase her fervour and courage to pursue a design so noble and divine, for which alone she was created; especially (3) considering the infinite danger of a negligent, tepid, and spiritually slothful life, and likewise the security and benefit of being but truly in the way to perfection, though she should never attain to it in this life.

First, therefore, to demonstrate that the way to perfection must needs be long and tedious, even to souls well-disposed thereto both by nature and education (for to others it is a way unpassable without extreme difficulty), this will easily be acknowledged by any well-minded soul that by her own experience will consider how obstinate, inflexible, and of how gluey and tenacious a nature corrupt self-love is in her; how long a time must pass before she can subdue any one habitual ill inclination and affection in herself. What fallings and risings again there are in our passions and corrupt desires, insomuch as when they seem to be quite mortified and almost forgotten, they will again raise themselves and combat us with as great or perhaps greater violence than before. Now till the poisonous root of self-love be withered, so as that we do not knowingly and deliberately suffer it to spring forth and bear fruit (for utterly killed it never will be in this life); till we have lost at least all affection to all our corrupt desires, even the most venial, which are almost infinite, perfect charity will never reign in our souls, and consequently perfect union in spirit with God cannot be expected; for charity lives and grows according to the measure that self-love is abated, and no further.

Souls that first enter into the internal ways of the spirit, or that have made no great progress in them, are guided by a very dim light, being able to discover and discern only a few grosser defects and inordinations; but by persevering in the exercises of mortification and prayer, this light will be increased, and then they will proportionably every day more and more discover a thousand secret and formerly invisible impurities in their intentions, self-seekings, hypocrisies, and close designs of nature, pursuing her own corrupt designs in the very best actions, cherishing nature one way when she mortifies it, and favouring price even when she exercises humility. Now a clear light to discover all these almost infinite deprivations not only in our sensitive nature, but also in the superior soul (which are far more secret, manifold, and dangerous), and a courage with success to combat and overcome them, must be the effect of a long-continued practice of prayer and mortification.

The want of a due knowledge or consideration hereof is the cause that some good souls, after they have made some progress in internal ways, becomes disheartened, and in danger to stop or quite leave them; for though at the first, being (as usually they are) prevented by God with a tender sensible devotion (which our Holy Father calls *fervorem novitium),* they do with much zeal and, as it seems to them, with good effect begin the exercises of mortification and prayer; yet afterward, such sensible fervour and tenderness ceasing (as it seldom fails to do) by that new light which they have gotten, they discern a world of defects, formerly undiscovered, which they erroneously think were not in them before; whereupon, fearing that instead of making progress, they are in a worse state than when they began, they will be apt to suspect that they are in a wrong way. This proceeds from a preconceived mistake, that because in times of light and devotion the soul finds herself carried with much fervour to God, and perceives but small contradictions and rebellions in inferior nature, therefore she is very forward in the way to perfection. Whereas it is far otherwise; for nature is not so easily conquered as she imagines, neither is the way to perfection so easy and short. Many changes she must expect; many risings and fallings; sometimes light, and sometimes darkness; sometimes calmness of passions, and presently after, it may be, fiercer combats than before; and these successions of changes repeated, God knows how oft, before the end approacheth.

Yea, it will likely happen to such souls, that even the formerly well-known grosser defects in them will seem to increase, and to grow more hard to be quelled after they have been competently advanced in internal ways; and the reason is, because, having set themselves to combat corrupt nature in all her perverse, crooked, and impure desires, and being sequestered from the vanities of the world, they find themselves in continual wrestlings and agonies, and want those pleasing diversions, conversations, and recreations, with which, whilst they lived a secular, negligent life, they could interrupt or put off their melancholic thoughts and unquietness. But if they would take courage and, instead of seeking ease from nature (further than discretion allows), have recourse for remedy by prayer to God, they would find that such violent temptations are an assured sign that they are in a secure and happy way, and that when God sees it is best for them, they shall come off from such combats with victory and comfort.

FOR SELF-EXAMINATION AND
JUDGE FOR YOURSELVES*
By Sören Kierkegaard

Sören Kierkegaard (1813-1855), raised in the Danish Lutheran church, rebelled against the conventional Christianity of his day. Christianity, in Kierkegaard's eyes, was a vital matter of individual conscience and not a social institution concerned with respectability. He believes everyone must rediscover himself as an individual alone before God. Christianity cannot be handed down in a tradition; every man who comes into this world must be shocked anew, and, in this shock, advance to faith or fall into despair. Indeed, Kierkegaard remains as one of the most vital shapers of twentieth century thought. Notice how Kierkegaard insists on dying to egoism before rising in spiritual awareness.

FOR SELF-EXAMINATION AND
JUDGE FOR YOURSELVES
It is the spirit which giveth life.

My hearer. With regard to Christianity, there is nothing to which every man is by nature more inclined than to take it in vain. There is nothing whatsoever in Christianity, not one solitary Christian definition, which may not, by undergoing a little alteration, merely by leaving out a subordinate determinant, becoming something entirely different, something of which it can be said that 'it has entered into the heart of man to believe'—and so it is taken in vain. On the other hand, there is nothing which Christianity has secured itself against with greater vigilance and zeal than against being taken in vain. There is absolutely no definition of Christian truth given without the subordinate determinant which is posited at the outset by Christianity, namely, death, this thing of dying—by which it would secure Christian truth against being taken in vain. They say, 'Christianity is gentle consolation, this is the gentle teaching of the grounds of consolation'—yes, that cannot be denied, if only one first will die, die from *(afdae)*; but that is not so gentle! They picture Christ, they say, 'Hear

*From Sören Kierkegaard, *For Self-Examination and Judge for Yourselves,* transl. with an Introduction and Notes, by Walter Lavine, published by Princeton University Press, 1944 (Princeton Paperback, 1968), pp. 95-106. Reprinted by permission of Princeton University Press.

His voice, how invitingly He calls all unto Him, all who suffer, and promises to give them rest for their souls'—and verily so it is, God forbid that I should say anything else; and yet, and yet, before this rest for the soul becomes thy portion, it is required (as the Inviter also says, and as His whole life here upon earth expresses, every blessed day and every blessed hour of the day) that thou must first die, die from—is this so inviting?

So it is also with this Christian truth: it is the Spirit which giveth life. To what feeling does a man cling tighter than to the vital feeling? What does he more strongly crave and more vehemently than to feel keenly the pulse of life in himself? What does he shudder at more than at dying? But here is preached a life-giving Spirit. So let us grasp at it. Who will hesitate? Give us life, more life, that the vital feeling may expand in me, as though all of life were gathered together in my breast!

But might this be what Christianity is, this dreadful error? No, no! This bestowing of life in the Spirit is not a *direct* increment of the natural life of man, *immediately* continuous with this—oh, blasphemy, oh, horror, thus to take Christianity in vain!—it is a new life. A new life, yes, and this is no mere phrase, as when the word is used for this or that, whenever something new begins to stir in us; no, a new life, literally a new life—for (observe this well!) death comes in between, this thing of being dead; and a life on the other side of death, yes, that is a new life.

Death comes in between, that is Christ's teaching, thou must die, precisely the life-giving Spirit is that which slays thee, this is the first expression of the life-giving Spirit, that thou must depart in death, that thou must die from *(afdoe)*[32]—this is in order that thou mayest not take Christianity in vain. A life-giving Spirit—that is the invitation. Who would not grasp at it? But die first—that gives us pause!

It is the Spirit which giveth life. Yes, it giveth life through death. For as it is said in an old hymn which would comfort the survivors for the loss of the deceased, 'With death we began to live,' so in a spiritual sense it is true that the communication of the life-giving Spirit begins with death. Think of today's festival! It was indeed a Spirit which makes alive which on this day was poured out upon the Apostles—and verily it was also a

32. It is time to remark that, although *do* and *afdo* both mean simply to die, the latter (literally, 'to die from') can be used metaphorically, as S.K. does here, in the sense of dying to self and to the world. An English translation is necessarily imperfect.

life-giving Spirit, as is shown by their life, by their death, whereof we have witness in the history of the Church, which came into existence precisely by the fact that the Spirit which giveth life was communicated to the Apostles. But what was their condition before this? Ah, who like the Apostles could teach what it is to die unto the world and unto themselves? For who has ever cherished such great expectations as for some time the Apostles were in a certain sense prompted to entertain? And whose expectations ever were so disappointed? Then came Easter morning, it is true, and Christ rose from the grave, and then came the Ascension—but then what further? Yes, he then was carried up to glory—but what then further? Oh, dost thou believe that any human, even the most audacious human hope could dare in the remotest way to engage in the task which was set the Apostles? No, here every merely human hope must despair. Then came the Spirit which made alive. So then the Apostles were dead, dead to every merely earthly hope, to every human confidence in their own power or in human assistance.

Therefore, first death, first thou must die to every merely earthly hope, to every merely human confidence, thou must die to thy selfishness or to the world; for it is only through thy selfishness that the world has power over thee; if thou hast died to thy selfishness, thou hast died also to the world. But, naturally, there is nothing a man clings to so tight as to his selfishness—which he clings to with his whole self! Ah, when in the hour of death soul and body are separated, it is not so painful as to be obliged to separate in one's lifetime from one's own soul! And a man does not cling so tight to his physical body as a man's selfishness clings to his selfishness! Let me take an example modelled after those old tales about what a man in more ancient times has experienced in the way of heart-felt sufferings, which these untried, sagacious times of ours will regard as a fable, possessing at most a little poetical value. Let us take an example, and to this end let me choose a subject about which we men talk so much and which employs us so much, I mean love. For love precisely is one of the strongest and deepest expressions of selfishness. So then think of a lover![33] He saw the object, and thereupon he fell in love. And this object

33. The 'lover' is S.K., and Regina is 'the object.' Anyone who knows S.K. from his Journals will recognize (as his contemporaries could not) how intimately personal this whole paragraph is. In one of his earliest books, *Fear and Trembling,* he had likened his sacrifice of Regina to Abraham's sacrifice of Isaac.

then became his eyes' delight and his heart's desire. And he grasped after it—it was his eyes' delight and his heart's desire! And he grasped it, he held it in his hand—it was his eyes' delight and his heart's desire! Then (so it goes in these old tales) a command was issued to him, 'Let go of this object!'—ah, and it was his eyes' delight and his heart's desire! My hearer, let us take pains to apprehend rightly how deep this shaft must penetrate if selfishness is really to be slain. For in his misery he cried, 'No, I will not let go, I cannot let go of this object; oh, have compassion upon me; if I may not retain it, well then, kill me, or at least let it be taken from me!' Thou canst well understand him; his selfishness would be wounded very deeply indeed by being deprived of the object, but he recognized justly that his selfishness would be still more deeply wounded if the requirement was that he should deprive himself of it. My hearer, let us go farther in order to follow the suffering into its deeper recesses when selfishness must be killed even more completely. Let us take the 'object' also into account. So then this object, which he had desired, which he grasped, of which he is in possession, his eyes' delight and his heart's desire, this object which he must let go, ah, his eyes' delight and his heart's desire, this object, let us assume for the sake of illuminating more strongly the pain of dying to it, this object is of the same opinion as he, that it would be cruel to sunder it from him—and it is he who must do this! He is to let go of that which no earthly power thinks of depriving him of, which now he finds it doubly difficult to let go, for (thou canst well imagine this) the object resorts to tears and prayers, invokes the living and the dead, both men and God, to prevent him—and he it is who must let go of this object! Here we have (if indeed he manages to get round that sharp corner without losing his senses)—here we have an example of what it is to die *(afdo)*. For not to see his wish, his hope, fulfilled, to be deprived of the object of his desire, his beloved—that may be very painful, selfishness is wounded, but that does not necessarily mean to die. No, but to be obliged to deprive oneself of the object of desire of which one is in possession—that is to wound selfishness at the root, as in the case of Abraham, when God required that Abraham himself, that he himself—frightful!—with his own hand—oh, horror of madness!—must sacrifice Isaac, Isaac, the gift so long and so lovingly expected, and the gift of God, for which Abraham conceived that he must give thanks his whole life long and would never be able to give thanks enough—Isaac, his only son, the son of his old age, and the son of promise. Dost thou believe that death can smart so painfully? I do not. And in any case, when it is a question of death, it is then all over with, but with this thing of 'dying from' it is by no means all over with, for he does not die, there lies perhaps a long life before him ... the deceased *(afdøde)*.

This is what it means to die. But before the Spirit can come which giveth life thou must first die. Ah, sometimes when for a day or for a longer period I have felt so indisposed, so weary, so incapacitated, so (this indeed is the way we express it) almost as if I were dead, then I too sighed within myself, 'Oh bring me life, life is what I need!' Or when perhaps I am taxed beyond my strength and discover, so I think, that I can hold out no longer; or when for a while it has been as if I had only misfortune in everything, and I sank down in despondency—then I have sighed within myself, 'Life, bring me life!' But from this it does not follow that Christianity is of the opinion that this is what I need. Suppose it held another opinion and said, 'No, first die completely; this is thy misfortune, that thou dost yet cling to life, to thy life which thou callest a torment and a burden, die completely!' I have seen a man sink almost into despair, I have also heard him cry out, 'Bring me life, life, this is worse than death which puts an end to life, whereas I am as dead and yet not dead!' I am not a severe man; if I knew any assuaging word, I should be very willing to comfort and cheer the man. And yet, and yet it is perfectly possible that what the sufferer had need of was really something else, that he needed harder sufferings. Harder sufferings! Who is the cruel one who ventures to say such a thing? My hearer, it is Christianity, the teaching which is offered at a selling-out price under the name of gentle comfort, whereas it—yes, verily, it is the comfort of eternity and for ever, but indeed it must take a rather hard hold. For Christianity is not what we men, both thou and I, are only too prone to make of it, it is not a quack. A quack is at your service right away, and right away applies the remedy, and bungles everything. Christianity waits before applying its remedy, it does not heal every wretched little ailment by means of eternity—this clearly is an impossibility as well as a self-contradiction—it heals by means of eternity and for ever when the sickness is such that eternity can be applied—that is to say, to this end thou must first die. Hence the severity of

Christianity, in order that it may not itself become twaddle (into which we men are so prone to transform it), and in order that it may not confirm thee in twaddle. And the rightness of this thou surely hast experienced in relation to smaller matters. Hast thou never had the experience—I have—that when perhaps thou hadst begun to moan and already to say, 'I can't endure it any longer,' then, the following day, when thou wast treated rather more sternly than ever—and then what? Then thou wast able to do it! When the horses groan and pant, thinking that they are jaded and that therefore a handful of hay is what they need—but when on the other hand, even with the halt of an instant the heavily loaded wagon would roll back to the brink and perhaps drag horse and driver and all with it into the abyss—is it then so cruel of the driver that the blows fall frightfully, frightfully, as he never had had the heart to beat that team of horses especially, which were to him (such a thing may well be true) like the apple of his eye—is that cruel, or is it loving? Is it cruel to be (if one will) cruel when this is absolutely the only thing that can save from destruction or help one through? So it is with dying *(at afdoe)*.

My hearer. Then, then cometh the life-giving Spirit. When? Why, when this has come to pass, when thou art deceased *(afdod)*; for as it is said, 'If we be dead with Christ, we shall also live with Him,' so also it may be said, 'If we are to live with Him, we must also die with Him.' First death, then life. But when? Well, when the first has come to pass; for with the coming of the life-giving Spirit it is as with the coming of the 'Comforter' which Christ promises the disciples. When comes the Comforter? He comes when all the dreadful things which Christ predicted of His own life have come first, and the like horrors which He predicted concerning the lives of the disciples—then comes the Comforter. And that He comes precisely at that same instant is not said; it is said only that it is when the first has come to pass, when this dying has occurred. Thus it is with the coming of the life-giving Spirit.

But it comes, it does not disappoint by failure to appear. Did it not come to the Apostles, did it disappoint them? Did it not come later to the true believers, did it disappoint them by failing to make an appearance?

No, it comes, and it brings the gifts of the Spirit: life and spirit.

It brings *faith*, 'faith,' that only being in the strictest sense faith which is the gift of the Holy Spirit after death has come between. For we men are not so precise in the use of words, we often speak of faith when in the strictest Christian sense it is not faith. In every man, with differences due to natural endowment, a stronger or weaker spontaneity (immediacy) is inborn. The stronger, the more vitally powerful it is, the longer it can hold out against opposition. And this power of resistance, this vital confidence in oneself, in the world, in mankind, and (among other things) in God, we call faith. But this is not using the word in a strictly Christian sense. Faith is against understanding, faith is on the other side of death. And when thou didst die, or didst die to thyself, to the world, thou didst at the same time die to all immediacy in thyself, and also to thine understanding. That is to say, when all confidence in thyself or in human support, and also in God as an immediate apprehension, when every probability is excluded, when it is dark as in the dark night—it is in fact death that we are describing—then comes the life-giving Spirit and brings faith. This strength is stronger than the whole world, it possesses the powers of eternity, it is the Spirit's gift from God, it is thy victory over the world, in which thou dost more than conquer.

And next the Spirit brings *Hope,* hope in the strictest Christian sense, this hope which is hope against hope. For in every man there is a spontaneous (immediate) hope, in one man it may be more vitally strong than in another, but in death (i.e. when thou dost die from) every such hope dies and transforms itself into hopelessness. Into this night of hopelessness—it is in fact death we are describing—comes then the life-giving Spirit and brings hope, the hope of eternity. It is against hope, for according to that merely natural hope there was no hope left, and so this is hope against hope. The understanding says, 'No, there is no hope'; thou, however, art dead to thine understanding, and in so far as that is the case it holds its peace, but if in any way it gets a chance to put in a word again, it will begin at once where it left off, 'there is no hope'—and it will surely deride this new hope, the Spirit's gift, just as the shrewd and understanding men who were gathered together at Pentecost derided the Apostles and said that they were full of new wine, just so will it deride thee and say to thee, 'Thou must have been drunk when such a thing occurred to thee, at least thou must have been out of thy wits'—there is none closer to knowing that than the understanding, and that is very understandingly said by the understanding, for to decease is also to die to the understanding, and the life-giving Spirit's hope is against the hope of the understanding. 'It is enough to drive one to despair,' says the understanding, 'however, that one can understand. But that on the other side of this (the fact that there is no hope) there should be a new hope, yea, the hope— that is, as surely as I call myself understanding, that is madness.' But the Spirit which giveth life (which the 'understanding' does not do) declares and bears witness: ' "The hope" is against hope.'

O thou who perhaps to the point of desperation art fighting hopelessly and in vain to find hope, it is this, it is not, which makes thee indignant, that in thine opinion thou canst absolutely victoriously make it evident even to a child or to the stupidest man that for thee there is no hope; and perhaps it is precisely this that embitters thee, that they will contradict this. Well then, entrust thyself to the Spirit, for with it thou canst talk, it acknowledges at once that thou art in the right, it says, 'That is quite right, and to me it is very important that this be insisted upon, for it is precisely from this that I, the Spirit, educe the proof that there is hope: hope against hope.' Canst thou require more? Canst thou think of any treatment better adapted to thy situation in suffering? It is granted that thou art in the right, that there is no hope; thou hast got the justice thou didst demand, and thou didst demand also to be what thou now art, to be spared all this prattle, all these loathsome grounds of consolation, thou art permitted, to thy great content, to be as sick as thou wilt without being disturbed by quacks, thou art permitted to do that which ends pain and quiets unrest, to turn away thy face and die, liberated from the baleful medical treatment of those who cannot bring new life but strive painfully to keep thee alive or hinder thee from dying—and in addition to all this thou dost get the 'hope' which is against hope, the Spirit's gift.

Finally, the Spirit also brings *love*. In other passages I have sought to show (what one cannot often enough lay stress upon, and never can make clear enough) that what we men extol under the name of love is selfishness, and that if we do not pay attention to this, the whole of Christianity becomes confusion to us.

Only when thou art dead to selfishness, and therewith to the world, so that thou dost not love the world, neither the things that are in the world, dost not even love selfishly a single person—when in love to God thou has learnt to hate thyself—only then can there be question of the love which is Christian love. According to our merely human conceptions, love coheres 'immediately' with our nature; we regard it as a matter of course therefore that it is strongest in the days of youth, when the heart possesses in immediacy all its warmth and enthusiasm, opens itself to others in devotion, responds to others in devotion. And so too we regard it, if not as a matter of course, yet as the usual course of things, that afterwards, as a man grows older, his nature attaches itself less to others, is closer, does not open itself so receptively, does not so openheartedly respond—which conviction we also explain as a sorry consequence of sorry experiences. 'Alas,' we say, 'for this glad heart of youth, of our own youth as well, so trusting, so devoted (if in fact this is exactly true!), was disappointed so often, so bitterly, I had to learn to know men from quite a different side, and therefore (so there is a therefore!) a good part of love was quenched also in my heart.'

Oh, my friend, how dost thou suppose the Apostles had learned to know man, does it seem to thee that it was from the favourable side? Verily, if ever there was any one (yet among those who are always afoot with much talk about this young, full, loving, friendly heart of youth, such a one is hardly to be found) who was justified in saying, 'I have so learned to know men that I am sure they do not deserve to be loved'—then it was Christ's Apostles! And this is an embittering experience; it is so natural to wish to find in men what one can love, and yet this is not an unreasonable experience when what is sought after is not the other's good, or not that alone. Not to find anything of the sort, to find the very opposite, and to find it on the scale the Apostles found it—ah, that is enough to be the death of one! And in a certain sense it was the death of the Apostles—they died, everything grew dark round about them (it is in fact death we are talking of!), when they had the frightful experience that love is not loved, that it is hated, that it is mocked, that it is spat upon, that it is crucified, in this world, and crucified while the justice which condemns it tranquilly washes its hands, and while the voice of the populace is loud for the robber. So surely they swore eternal enmity to this unloving world? Ah, yes, in a certain sense, but in another aspect, no, no; in their love for God, in order that they might abide in love, they banded themselves, so to speak, together with God to love this unloving world—the life-giving Spirit brought them love. And so the Apostles resolved, in likeness with the Pattern, to love, to suffer, to be sacrificed, for the sake of saving the unloving world. And this is love.

Such gifts the life-giving Spirit brought to the Apostles at Pentecost—oh, that the Spirit would also bring such gifts to us, there is verily great need of this in our times.

My hearer, I have still a word I would say; but I will clothe it in a form of presentation which perhaps at the first glance will seem to thee less solemn. I do it, however, advisedly and intentionally, because I think that in this way it will make a truer impression upon thee.

Once upon a time there was a rich man who ordered from abroad at a high price a pair of entirely faultless and high-bred horses which he desired to have for his own pleasure and for the pleasure of driving them himself. Then about a year or two elapsed. Anyone who previously had known these horses would not have been able to recognize them again. Their eyes had become dull and drowsy, their gait lacked style and decision, they couldn't endure anything, they couldn't hold out, they hardly could be driven four miles without having to stop on the way, sometimes they came to a standstill as he sat for all he was worth attempting to drive them, besides they had acquired all sorts of vices and bad habits, and in spite of the fact that they of course got fodder in over-abundance, they were falling off in flesh day by day. Then he had the King's coachman called. He drove them for a month—in the whole region there was not a pair of horses that held their heads so proudly, whose glance was so fiery, whose gait was so handsome, no other pair of horses that could hold out so long, though it were to trot for more than a score of miles at a stretch without stopping. How came this about? It is easy to see. The owner, who without being a coachman pretended to be such, drove them in accordance with the horses' understanding of what it is to drive; the royal coachman drove them in accordance with the coachman's understanding of what it is to drive.

So it is with us men. Oh, when I think of myself and of the countless men I have learnt to know, I have often said to myself despondently, 'Here are talents and powers and capacities enough—but the coachman is lacking.' Through a long period of time, we men, from generation to generation, have been, if I may so say, driven (to stick to the figure) in accordance with the horses' understanding of what it is to drive, we are directed, brought up, educated in accordance with man's conception of what it is to be a man. Behold therefore what we lack: exaltation, and what follows in turn from this, that we only can stand so little, impatiently employ at once the means of the instant, and in our impatience desire instantly to see the reward of our labour, which just for this reason is deferred.

Once it was different. Once there was a time when it pleased the Deity (if I may venture to say so) to be Himself the coachman; and He drove the horses in accordance with the coachman's understanding of what it is to drive. Oh, what was a man not capable of at that time!

Think of today's text! There sit twelve men, all of them belonging to that class of society which we call the common people. They had seen Him whom they adored as God, their Lord and Master, crucified; as never could it be said of anyone even in the remotest, it can be said of them that they had seen everything lost. It is true, He thereupon went triumphantly to heaven—but in this way also He is lost to them: and now they sit and wait for the Spirit to be imparted to them, so that thus, execrated as they are by the little nation they belong to, they may preach a doctrine which will arouse against them the hate of the whole world, that is the task; these twelve men are to transform the world—and that on the most terrible terms, against its will. Truly, here the understanding is brought to a standstill! In order now, so long after, to form merely a faint conception of it, the understanding is brought to a standstill—supposing that one has any understanding; it is as if one were to lose one's understanding—supposing one has any understanding to lose.

It is Christianity that had to be put through. These twelve men, they put it through. They were in a sense men like us—but they were well driven, yea, they were well driven!

Then came the next generation. They put Christianity through. They were men just like us—but they were well driven! Yea, verily, that they were! It was with them as with that pair of horses when the royal coachman drove them. Never has a man ever lifted his head so proudly in loftiness above the world as the first Christians did in humility before God! And just as that pair of horses could trot, even if it were for a score of miles or more, without being pulled up to give them breath, so these ran, they ran at one stretch for three score years and ten without getting out of harness, without being pulled up anywhere; no, proud as they were in humility before God, they said, 'It is not for us to lie down and dawdle on the way, we come to a stop first . . . at eternity!' It was Christianity that had to be put through; so they put it through, yea, that they did; but they also were well driven, yea, that they were!

O Holy Spirit—we pray for ourselves and for all—oh, Holy Spirit, Thou who dost make alive; here it is not talents we stand in need of, nor culture, nor shrewdness, rather there is here too much of all that; but what we need is that Thou take away the power of mastery and give us life. True it is that a man experiences a shudder like that of death when Thou, to become the power in him, dost take the power from him—oh, but if even animal creatures understand at a subsequent moment how well it is for them that the royal coachman took the reins, which in the first instance prompted them to shudder, and against which their mind rebelled—should not then a man be able promptly to understand what a benefaction it is towards a man that Thou takest away the power and givest life?

Maturing in Faith

Part II

MATURING IN FAITH

One can hardly read a page of the writings of the great mystics without finding a constant reiteration of the necessity of detachment, renunciation and self-mortification, if any progress in the spiritual life is to be made. Perhaps the most perennial question asked of the spiritual life is why one must proceed through this purgation or purifying process to find God.

Spiritual writers attempt to answer this question in stating that mankind in Adam was unified in himself since all his faculties were concentrated on God alone. However, with Adam's fall mankind fell from this loving union—from this "one-ing affection"—and was scattered over creatures so that to love God became impossible. The aim of spirituality is to return to that state of original justice in which, before sin, all man's faculties were united in contemplating God. The spiritual road is then the work of the Holy Spirit leading the wayward soul back to the perfection to which it was originally called. This work is only possible because of the reconciliation wrought for man's redemption by Christ.

Spiritual writers additionally assert that the ego of which we are normally conscious is not the true self. The ego is only the ephemeral, phenomenal self that is subject to moods, changes and tastes. In man there is another self, the true self or spirit which is not affected by rdinary happenings. This spirit is constant, immortal a unchanging. It is in his spirit that man has contact with God this is man's divine essence without which there could be no union between God and man. It is through the mystical experience that man becomes aware of his spiritual nature. Hitherto, sin had obscured such knowledge. The aim of the spiritual life is for one to discover his true self and thus become one in spirit and love with God.

Fallen man is unable to find peace in anything but God. St. Augustine claims that our hearts are restless until they rest in Him. The earthly desires men cherish are mere illusion. Why then are they pursued? Because the pursuit itself has become the substitute for contemplation. Unable to rest in anything achieved, man forgets his discontent in a ceaseless quest for new satisfactions. In this pursuit, desire itself becomes the chief satisfaction. A life based on desires is like a spider's web, says St. Gregory of Nyssa. Woven about us by the father of lies, the devil, the enemy of our souls, it is a frail tissue of vanities without substance, and yet it can catch us and hold us fast, delivering us up to him as his prisoner. Each generation is condemned by nature to wear itself out in the pursuit of illusions that cannot satisfy. Man exhausts himself in the pursuit of mirages that ever fade and are renewed as fast as they have faded.[34]

Man was made for the restful activity of contemplation but sin robbed him of his spiritual birthright. Man's incapacity for this one deep activity which is the very reason for his existence, is precisely what drives him to seek oblivion in exterior motion and desire. Man's preoccupation with trifles serves as a dope; it will blur his sense of who he is and what he was made for. Pascal once remarked that distraction is the only thing that consoles us for our miseries and yet it is, itself, the greatest of our miseries. One cannot find the true light unless the false be darkened. One cannot find peace unless illusion is deprived. Peace is found by detaching oneself from that which imprisons the spirit. This detachment rather than ascetical self-denials is the meaning of spiritual suffering.[35]

In spiritual growth there is no special method of prayer or austerity but rather an emphasis on keeping the heart of the disciple open to love and to prevent it from hardening in self-centered spiritual or physical concern. All the worst sins are denials and refusals to love. The chief aim of spiritual direction is to teach the disciple not to sin against love and then to encourage and assist his growth in love until he becomes divinized. One who grows spiritually surrenders himself to the demands of the Gospel and to Evangelical charity, totally forgetting himself in obedience to the Spirit of God so that he lives as a Christian.[36] Ego surrender culminates in the discovery of the true self, then as St. Paul exclaims: "I live, no not I, but Christ lives within me."

There are two reading divisions within this chapter. The first eight selections relate to the necessity of maturing out of one's closed world in order that one may experience the liberation of the resurrected Christ. The object of sanctification is to experience spiritual fulfillment if only partially in this life. God is willing to give but are men willing to forgo illusion for reality?

---

34. Thomas Merton, *The Ascent to Truth*, (New York: Viking Press, 1951), p. 24-25.
35. *Ibid.*, p. 26.
36. Thomas Merton, *Mystics and Zen Masters*, (New York: Dell Pub. Co., 1967), p. 186.

Within the first division of readings, selections are taken from Scripture wherein St. Paul is preeminent. Paul is Christianity's first witness to the progressive degrees of sanctification. Paul's epistles if read in chronological order note his continuous mystical development. The second author, Catherine of Genoa, depicts how human nature is in conflict with spiritual reality and why this is so. Meister Eckhart and his two disciples, Henry Suso and John Tauler follow. Eckhart is the father of German mysticism and a giant in the field of spirituality. His writings are the springboard for the Rhineland school of Renaissance spirituality. Both the romantic Suso and the reformer Tauler apply Eckhartian principles with their own insights in their writings. Gregory of Nyssa, represents the best of the fathers in the development of spiritual thought. His short excerpt is succinct on the need of detachment from illusion to find the bridegroom of the soul. Next is Walter Hilton, already mentioned in the previous selection. Hilton surveys the whole gamut of spirituality from the leap of faith through reformation in feeling or contemplation. His following little parable of the pilgrim is classic in the insights he gives on the spiritual road. The last writing of pre-mysticism is from Watchman Nee, a twentieth century Chinese evangelical Protestant. His demands for surrender to the workings of the Holy Spirit are in agreement with the traditional ancient and medieval beliefs. Nee, a prolific writer, is currently quite popular and has traveled far on the road of sanctification.

The next three readings deal with the first mystical encounter and its further purifications. Few spiritual writers can compete with St. Teresa in captivating the first union experience with God. The initial union experiences are like the physical plane of the first meeting with one's marriage partner. Ecstasy is the betrothal or engagement described in the next chapter. The initial mystic meeting is revolutionary in its implications. It makes one a contemplative; God is seen as the cause and purpose of creation and that man's ultimate fulfillment can be had only in Him. Yet even at this stage man's donation of his will to the divine is not complete. The union experience is to strengthen man's spirit for its still further goal of stripping itself of its ego in order to discover his divinity.

St. John of the Cross, a friend of St. Teresa and one of

Christianity's greatest mystics, describes the purgations after the initial mystical experiences. He labels the continuing purifications the "dark night of the soul." The last selection is from Simone Weil, an unbaptized Christian of this century. She relates the meaning of suffering in imitating the total self-surrender of Christ.

SCRIPTURE*

The basic mystic ideas embodied in the New Testament are found in the Johannine writings and the epistles of St. Paul. Since the epistles were written before the Gospels, the earliest documentary witness to Christ is the witness of mysticism of St. Paul. St. Paul is the first and one of the greatest of the Christian mystics. The following selections advance the idea of confirmity with Jesus before liberation will be had.

SCRIPTURE

Your protest, your battle against sin, has not yet called for bloodshed; yet you have lost sight, already, of those words of comfort in which God addresses you as his sons; My son, do not undervalue the correction which the Lord sends thee, do not be unmanned when he reproves thy faults. It is where he loves that he bestows correction; there is no recognition for any child of his, without chastisement. Be patient, then, while correction lasts; God is treating you as his children. Was there ever a son whom his father did not correct?

Hebrews 12, 4-7

Being what thou art, lukewarm, neither cold nor hot, thou wilt make me vomit thee out of my mouth. I am rich, thou sayest, I have come into my own; nothing, now, is wanting to me. And all the while, if thou didst but know it, it is thou who art wretched, thou who art to be pitied. Thou art a beggar, blind and naked; and my counsel to thee is, to come and buy from me what thou needest; gold, proved in the fire, to make thee rich, and white garments, to clothe thee, and cover up the nakedness which dishonours thee; rub salve, too, upon thy eyes, to restore them sight. It is those I love that I correct and chasten; kindle thy generosity, and repent. See where I stand at the door, knocking; if anyone listens to my voice and opens the door, I will come in to visit him, and take my supper with him, and he shall sup with me. Who wins the victory? I will let him share my throne with me; I too have won the victory, and now I sit sharing my Father's throne. Listen, you that have ears, to the message the Spirit has for the churches.

Apocalypse 3, 16-22

*The following excerpts are taken from *Good News for Modern Man,* American Bible Society, 1971.

And you must not fall in with the manners of this world; there must be an inward change, a remaking of your minds, so that you can satisfy yourselves what is God's will, the good thing, the desirable thing, the perfect thing.

Romans 12, 2

You must put aside, then, every trace of ill will and deceitfulness, your affectations, the grudges you bore, and all the slanderous talk; you are children new-born, and all your craving must be for the soul's pure milk, that will nurture you into salvation, once you have tasted, as you have surely tasted, the goodness of the Lord. Draw near to him; he is the living antitype of that stone which men rejected, which God has chosen and prized; you too must be built up on him, stones that live and breathe, into a spiritual fabric; you must be a holy priesthood, to offer up that spiritual sacrifice which God accepts through Jesus Christ .... You are a chosen race, a royal priesthood, a consecrated nation, a people God means to have for himself; it is yours to proclaim the exploits of the God who has called you out of darkness into his marvellous light.

I Peter 2, 1-5; 9

For this reason we never become discouraged. Even though our physical being is gradually decaying, yet our spiritual being is renewed day after day. And this small and temporary trouble we suffer will bring us a tremendous and eternal glory, much greater than the trouble. For we fix our attention, not on things that are seen, but on things that are unseen. What can be seen lasts only for a time; but what cannot be seen lasts forever.

For we know that when this tent we live in—our body here on earth—is torn down, God will have a house in heaven for us to live in, a home he himself made, which will last forever. And now we sigh, so great is our desire to have our home which is in heaven.

II Corinthians 4:16-18
5: 1-2

For his sake I have thrown everything away; I consider it all as mere garbage, so that I might gain Christ, and be completely united with him. No longer do I have a righteousness of my own, the kind to be gained by obeying the Law. I now have the righteousness that is given through faith in Christ, the righteousness that comes from God, and is based on faith. All I want is to know Christ and to experience the power of his resurrection; to share in his sufferings and become like him in his death, in the hope that I myself will be raised from death to life.   *Philippians* 3:8-11

Now that we have been put right with God through faith, we have peace with God through our Lord Jesus Christ. He has brought us, by faith, into this experience of God's grace, in which we now live. We rejoice, then, in the hope we have of sharing God's glory! And we also rejoice in our troubles, because we know that trouble produces endurance, endurance brings God's approval, and his approval creates hope. This hope does not disappoint us, because God has poured out his love into our hearts by means of the Holy Spirit, who is God's gift to us.   *5 Romans* 1-5

I consider that what we suffer at this present time cannot be compared at all with the glory that is going to be revealed to us. All of creation waits with eager longing for God to reveal his sons. For creation was condemned to become worthless, not of its own will, but because God willed it to be so. Yet there was this hope, that creation itself would one day be set free from its slavery to decay, and share the glorious freedom of the children of God. For we know that up to the present time all of creation groans with pain like the pain of childbirth. But not just creation alone; we who have the Spirit as the first of God's gifts, we also groan within ourselves as we wait for God to make us his sons and set our whole being free. For it was by hope that we were saved; but if we see what we hope for, then it is not really hope. For who hopes for something that he sees? But if we hope for what we do not see, we wait for it with patience.

In the same way the Spirit also comes to help us, weak that we are. For we do not know how we ought to pray; the Spirit himself pleads with God for us, in groans that words cannot express. And God, who sees into the hearts of men, knows what the thought of the Spirit is; because the Spirit pleads with God on behalf of his people and in accordance with his will.

We know that in all things God works for good with those who love him, those whom he has called according to his purpose. Those whom God had already chosen he had also set apart to become like his Son, so that the Son would be the first among many brothers. And so God called those that he had set apart; and those that he called he also put right with himself; and with those that he put right with himself he also shared his glory.

Faced with all this, what can we say? If God is for us, who can be against us? He did not even keep back his own Son, but offered him for us all! He gave us his Son—will he not also freely give us all things? Who will accuse God's chosen people? God himself declares them not guilty! Can anyone, then, condemn them? Christ Jesus is the one who died, or rather, who was raised to life and is at the right side of God. He pleads with God for us! Who, then, can separate us from the love of Christ? Can trouble do it, or hardship, or persecution, or hunger, or poverty, or danger, or death? As the scripture says,

> "For your sake we are in danger of death
>> the whole day long;
>> we are treated like sheep that are going
>> to be slaughtered."

No, in all these things we have complete victory through him who loved us! For I am certain that nothing can separate us from his love; neither death nor life, neither angels nor other heavenly rulers or powers; neither the present nor the future; neither the world above nor the world below—there is nothing in all creation that will ever be able to separate us from the love of God which is ours through Christ Jesus our Lord.

8 Romans 18-39

THE LIFE AND SAYINGS OF
ST. CATHERINE OF GENOA*
ed. by Paul Garvin

The life and work of St. Catherine of Genoa are little known. She was married and devoted much of her time to hospital work. She was a mystic who has left some timeless wisdom for one developing in the spiritual life. She died just before the Reformation. The following are excerpts from her writings. Notice how she separates the true from the false self.

THE LIFE AND SAYINGS OF
ST. CATHERINE OF GENOA
The false self: self-love and self-will

Ch. XIV

Man was created for the end of possessing happiness. Having deviated from this his end, he has become deformed by making for himself a self which in all things struggles against the soul's true happiness. Hence it is necessary for us all to submit to God this self of ours, which does all it can to fill our minds with obstacles to our straight progress. God must consume it till nothing is left but Himself, else the soul cannot find firmness or contentment, not having been created for any other end. Hence it is that, when He can do so, God draws the free will of man to Himself with gentle enticements; and when He has done so, He so arranges it that He can lead it to the annihilation of its self.

Ch. XXXI

All sufferings, displeasures and pains are caused by attachment to the false self. Although adversities may often seem to us to be unreasonable, because of certain considerations which we believe to be true and indeed quite evident, yet the fact is that it is our own imperfection that does not allow us to see the truth, and this is the reason why we feel pain, suffering and displeasure.

Ch. XXV

Self-love has these conditions: firstly, it pays no heed to the harm to soul or body, or to its neighbor, or to its reputation or

*Reprinted with permission of Alba House, New York, N.Y. 1964 from *The Life and Sayings of St. Catherine of Genoa*, pp. 100-103.

possessions or those of others. To satisfy its own will it is cruel to itself and to others. It will not yield to any opposition that can be thought of, and when it has resolved on doing something, it will not change with flattery or threats of any disasters however great. To carry out its purpose it takes no account of servitude, poverty, disgrace, infirmity, death, purgatory or hell, for it is so blind they do not matter to it.

If you said to a man: Leave your self-love and you will gain money, live in health, and have everything the heart can desire in this world, and when you die go to heaven as well, he would reject it all, for his heart can value nothing except what he has resolved from self-love. He mocks at all else and holds it as nothing. Like a slave, he lets himself be led by it where and how it wills, and is so submissive to it that he can hardly wish for anything else. He neither speaks nor thinks nor cares about anything else, and if someone says to him: 'You are mad, what you are doing is wrong,' he will not listen, nor is he offended if he is mocked at. He has shut his eyes and stopped his ears to all else, and nothing else matters to him.

Ch. XII

Our self-will is so subtle and so deeply-rooted within us, so covered with excuses and defended by false reasoning that it seems a devil. When we cannot do our own will in one way, we do it in another, under all kinds of pretexts—of charity, of necessity, of justice, of perfection, or of suffering for God's sake, or of finding spiritual consolation, or of health, or from the example of others, or of pleasing someone who is trying to oblige us.

Ch. XXV

Self-love is so skillful a thief that it steals even from God without remorse or self-reproach. It does so as if it were taking something of its own, without which it could not live, and had a claim to it from right and necessity. It cloaks its actions under the pretense of good, and it is impossible to prove the contrary except by the penetrating light of true love, which asserts its will to stand naked without any covering, as it has nothing shameful to hide.

As self-love cannot know what naked love is, so naked love cannot understand how it is possible there should be anything of its own in the things it truly knows. Naked love always sees the truth and can see nothing but the truth, while self-love can neither see it nor believe in it. Believing itself to have it, it considers the real truth an enemy, or a stranger and an alien.

Ch. XXV

Self-love is the root of all the misfortunes that can happen to us in this world and the next. I see the example of Lucifer, who is in the state he is in for having made this perverted love his object. I see it still better in ourselves, and where Adam has brought us to with this germ of his, and which man's veins, nerves and bones are so full that he cannot say, do or think anything that is not full of this poisonous love.

Ch. XVI

I wish to draw near to God, so I am in every way bound to be an enemy of His enemies. And as I can find nothing that is more of an enemy to Him than my own self, I am obliged to hate this part of me more than any other thing. Because of the opposition between it and the spirit, I am determined to separate it from all that is good in this world and the next, and hold it in no more consideration than if it did not exist.

Ch. XIII

I know that all that is in us of self must be destroyed until there is nothing left of it. This is because of its malignity, which is such that it can only be overcome by God's goodness. Unless He hides it and destroys it in Himself, it would never be possible for us to shake off what is worse than hell. Every day I see more clearly how horrible is the natural self. Anyone who had no trust in God's providence would despair if he saw how frightful we are in comparison with God, who with great love and care seeks continually to help us.

Ch. XX

God is ever ready to give us all the means necessary for us to be saved, and is ever attentive to all we do, only for our own good. Man, on the other hand, is ever occupied in useless things, opposed to his true self and of no value. At the time of death God will say to him: 'What could I do for you, O man, that I did not do?' Then man will see this clearly, and will render a stricter account for it than for all his other sins.

Ch. XX

O man, formed into a creature of such dignity, why do you waste your time in the pettiness of such worthless things? If you consider well, you would easily recognize that all you can desire and have in the present life is nothing in comparison with the spiritual things that are given by God. If these are given in this life, full of ignorance as it is, what will it be like in that heavenly home, where there are things that the eye has not seen nor the ear heard, nor are imagined in the heart of man, which God has prepared for those who love Him?

THE CLOUD OF UNKNOWING*
Trans. by Ira Progoff

The author of this famous English classic is not known. He was probably a religious who lived during the fourteenth century, the golden age of English mysticism. The curious title of his book means that between God and man there is a mystery (cloud). Although the cloud remains, God manifests Himself by love to the responsive soul. This selection is intended to show the difficulties inherent in the spiritual life and to give one encouragement for the journey.

THE CLOUD OF UNKNOWING
That a man should continue patiently in this work, enduring its pain and judging no man

Whoever desires, therefore, to reach the purity that has been lost by sin and to achieve that state of well-being in which there is no pain must necessarily labor in this work with great patience, enduring the pains of it no matter how great they be, whether he has been a habitual sinner or not.

Everyone finds it difficult to do this work, both sinners and innocent people who have hardly sinned at all. But those who have been sinners have much greater difficulty, and for good reason. It often happens, however, that some who have been serious and habitual sinners reach perfection in this work sooner than those who have not been sinners. This is the merciful miracle of our Lord who bestows His grace in ways that arouse the wonderment of the world.

How the work of this book is to be carried out and its value beyond all other works

This is the work of the soul that is most pleasing to God. All the saints and angels rejoice in this work and they do all that is in their power to assist it. By contrast, all the demons will be furious at your doing this work, and they will try to defeat it in every way they can. All of mankind living on earth will be helped by this work in wonderful ways of which you are not even aware.

---

*Taken from *The Cloud of Unknowing* by Ira Progoff. © 1957 by Ira Progoff. Used by permission of the Julian Press, a division of Crown Publishers, Inc., pp. 130, 61, 62, 65.

Do not slacken, therefore, but persevere in the work until you feel the desire. For, when you begin it, you will find that there is at the start but a darkness; there is, as it were, a cloud of unknowing. You know not what it is except that you feel in your will a naked intent toward God.

No matter what you do, this darkness and this cloud is between you and your God and because of it you can neither see Him clearly with your reason in the light of understanding, nor can you feel Him with your affection in the sweetness of love. Be prepared, therefore, to remain in this darkness as long as must be, crying evermore for Him whom you love. For if you are ever to feel Him or to see Him, it will necessarily be within this cloud and within this darkness. And if you will work with great effort as I bid you, I trust in His mercy that you will achieve it.

For this reason, whoever has been transformed by grace so that he follows this way of obeying the urgings of his will should not remain in this life without some taste of the infinite sweetness; for, just as he is not without these urgings in nature, so he may not be in the bliss of heaven without the full food.

Do not wonder, therefore, that I urge you on to this work. For this is a work, as you shall learn in a little while, that man would have continued to do if he had never sinned. And it was for this work that man was made, as all things also were made to help him and further him in this work, so that by means of it man shall be made whole again. And by failing to carry out this work, a man falls ever deeper and deeper into sin and is drawn ever further and further away from God. But by holding to this work and working in it continually, a man rises ever higher and higher away from sin and comes closer and closer to God.

MEISTER ECKHART: A MODERN TRANSLATION*
By Raymond Blankney

The father of German mysticism is Meister Eckhart, a thirteenth century Dominican. He ranks with the greatest of the Christian mystics whose experiences with God has quickened other souls, and through them enriched the general Christian consciousness. He preached to those who could bear it and his immense reputation testifies to the general hunger for a deepening of spiritual life that he was able to fill. His brilliant insights would affect future German mystics. The following are fragments from his writings.

FRAGMENTS

Our Lord said to Zacchaeus: "Make haste and come down; for today I must abide at thy house." If anyone wants to see Jesus, he must outstrip the world of things; but if one does not get beyond the world of things, what does that mean? It means that one has never tasted God, for if he had, he would make haste to excel the world, to burst through creatures. One bursts through creatures when he lets go of things he has loved.

That we are not able to see God is due to the faintness of desire and the throng of things. To desire high things is to be high. To see God, one must desire high: know that earnest desire and deep humility work wonders. I say that God can do anything, but he cannot deny anything to the person who is humble and yet has high desires and so, if I cannot compel God to do what I want him to do, then I fail either in humility or in desire. I swear it, for I am certain that a man who wanted to do so, might one day be able to walk through a wall of steel, or do, as we read of St. Peter, that when he laid eyes on Jesus, he walked on water in his eagerness to meet him.

Now I say that a vessel that grows as it is filled will never be full. If a bin able to hold a cartload grew while you were dumping your load in it, you could never fill it. The soul is like that: the more it wants the more it is given; the more it receives the more it grows.

Who is Jesus? He has no name.

*From pp. 233-237 and 246-250 in *Meister Eckhart: A Modern Translation* by Raymond Bernard Blankney, Copyright 1941 by Harper & Row, Publishers, Inc. Reprinted by permission of the publisher.

Meister Eckhart said in a sermon: God's divinity comes of my humility, and this may be demonstrated as follows. It is God's peculiar property to give; but he cannot give unless something is prepared to receive his gifts. If, then, I prepare by my humility to receive what he gives, by my humility I make God a giver. Since it is his nature to give, I am merely giving God what is already his own. It is like a rich man who wants to be a giver but must first find a taker, since without a taker he cannot be a giver; for the taker, in taking, makes the rich man a giver. Similarly, if God is to be a giver, he must first find a taker, but no one may be a taker of God's gifts except by his humility. Therefore, if God is to exercise his divine property by his gifts, he well may need my humility; for apart from humility he can give me nothing—without it I am not prepared to receive his gift. That is why it is true that by humility I give divinity to God.

Meister Eckhart also said: Humility exalts God and the more I have it, the more he is exalted and the more gently and sweetly his divine influence and gifts flow into me.

That God is exalted by humility, I argue thus: The more I abase myself, the higher God rises above me. Humility is like a well. The deeper the well the higher he will stand who stands on the top. Similarly, the deeper I dig down into humility the more exalted God becomes and the more gently and sweetly his divine influence pours into me. That is why I must exalt God by humility.

The question has been raised as to whether it is possible to make the senses obey the mind.

Meister Eckhart answered it by saying: If the mind is fixed on God and continues so, the senses will obey it. It is like hanging a needle on a magnet and then another needle onto that, and so on. It might even be possible to suspend four needles from the magnet in this way. As long as the first needle hangs onto the magnet, the rest will hang onto it, but if the first drops off, it will lose the rest. And so, as long as the mind is firmly fixed on God, the senses will obey it but when the mind drops away from God, the senses drop off from the mind and are unruly.

Meister Eckhart said: The person whose attitude varies from one thing to another, to whom God is dearer in one form than another, is crude, uninstructed, and a child. To see God evenly in everything is to be a man; but that person has really arrived to whom all creatures are merely bypaths to exile.

He was also asked if a person who denies himself need care at all what happens otherwise. He replied: God's yoke is easy and his burden is light. He asks of us only the willingness. What comes hard to the apprentice is a delight to the master. The Kingdom of God is for none but those who are thoroughly dead [to the world].

Meister Eckhart said: I shall never pray that God give me himself. I shall pray that he make me pure; for if I am pure, God must give himself and dwell in me, because it is his peculiar nature to do so.

Meister Eckhart spoke this way: One person who has mastered life is better than a thousand persons who have mastered only the contents of books, but no one can get anything out of life without God. If I were looking for a master of learning, I should go to Paris to the colleges where the higher studies are pursued, but if I wanted to know about the perfection of life, they could not tell me there.

Where, then, should I go? To [someone who has] a nature that is pure and free and nowhere else: there I should find the answer for which I so anxiously inquire. People, why do you search among the dead bones? Why don't you look for life eternal in life's holy places? The dead can neither give nor take. If an angel had to seek God without God, he would look for him in a pure, free, disinterested creature and nowhere else. Perfection depends only on accepting poverty, misery, hardship, disappointment, and whatever comes in course, and accepting it willingly, gladly, freely, eagerly until death, as if one were prepared for it and therefore unmoved by it and not asking why.

Meister Eckhart said in a sermon, when asked what the birth of God is: The birth of God in the soul is simply God revealing himself in some new bit of knowledge which has taken a new form.

Again he was asked if the soul's highest blessedness came with the spiritual birth of God in man. He replied: Even though God gets more pleasure from this act than any other thing he does to any creature in heaven or on earth, the soul is more blessed when it is reborn into him. The soul is not blessed perfectly when God is born in it but rather when, with love and praise, it follows the revelation of God back to the source from whence it came, their common origin, letting go of its own things and cleaving to his, so that the soul is blessed by God's things and not its own.

Meister Eckhart says: The Holy Scriptures shout that man should be free from self, for being freed from self, you are self-controlled, and as you are self-controlled you are self-possessed, and as you are self-possessed you possess God and all creation. I tell you the truth, as sure as God is God and I am man, if you could be freed from self—as free as you are of the highest angels—then you would have the nature of the highest angels as completely as you now have your own. By this discipline, man becomes master of himself.

Meister Eckhart said: Grace comes only with the Holy Spirit. It carries the Holy Spirit on its back. Grace is not a stationary thing; it is always found in a Becoming. It can only flow out of God and then only immediately. The function of grace is to transform and reconvey [the soul] to God. Grace makes the soul godlike. God, the core of the soul, and grace belong together.

To get at the core of God at his greatest, one must first get into the core of himself at his least, for no one can know God who has not first known himself. Go to the depths of the soul, the secret place of the Most High, to the roots, to the heights; for all that God can do is focused there.

The just man lives in God and God in him, for God is born in him and he in God. With each virtue of the just person, God is born and made glad, and not only with each virtue, but with each deed, however trifling, done out of virtue and justice, and resulting in justice, God is made glad—glad through and through!—so that there is nothing in the core of the Godhead that does not dance for joy! Ordinary persons can only believe this; but the enlightened know it.

When the soul so lives in its own secret place that it is the image of God, then it has true unity that no creature can divide. God, the angels, and creatures to the contrary notwithstanding, nothing can separate this soul from the image of God. This is true unity, and true blessedness depends on it.

Our Lord cannot endure that any who love him should be worried, for fear is painful. Thus St. John says: "Love casteth out fear." Love cannot put up with either fear or pain, and so, to grow in love is to diminish in fear, and when one has become a perfect lover, fear has gone out of him altogether.

At the beginning of a good life, however, fear is useful. It is love's gateway. A punch or an awl makes a hole for the thread with which a shoe is sewed . . . and a bristle is put on the thread to get it through the hole, but when the thread does bind the shoe together, the bristle is out. So fear leads love at first and when love has bound us to God, fear is done away.

Meister Eckhart's good friends bade him: "Since you are going to leave us, give us one last word."

"I will give you," he replied, "a rule which is the stronghold of all I have ever said, in which are lodged all the truths to be discussed or put into practice."

It often happens that what seems trivial to us is more important to God than what we think important. Therefore, we ought to take everything God puts on us evenly, not comparing and wondering which is more important, or higher, or best. We ought simply to follow where God leads, that is, to do what we are most inclined to do, to go where we are repeatedly admonished to go—to where we feel most drawn. If we do that, God gives us his greatest in our least and never fails.

Now, some people despise the little things of life. It is their mistake, for they thus prevent themselves from getting God's greatness out of these little things. God is every way, evenly in all ways, to him who has the eyes to see. But sometimes it is hard to know whether one's inclinations come from God or not, but that can be decided this way: If you find yourself always possessed of a knowledge or intimation of God's will, which you obey before everything else, because you feel urged to obey it and the urge is frequent, then you may know that it is from God.

Some people want to recognize God only in some pleasant enlightenment—and then they get pleasure and enlightenment but not God. Somewhere it is written that God shines in the darkness where every now and then we get a glimpse of him. More often, God is where his light is least apparent. Therefore we ought to expect God in all manners and all things evenly.

Someone may now say: I should be glad to look for God evenly in all shapes and things, but my mind does not always work the same way—and then, not as well with this as with that. To which I reply: That is too bad! All paths lead to God and he is on them all evenly, to him who knows. I am well aware that a person may get more out of one technique than another but it is not best so. God responds to all techniques evenly to a knowing man. Such and such may be the way, but it is not God.

But even if God is in all ways and all things evenly, do I not still need a special way to get to him? Let us see. Whatever the way that leads you most frequently to awareness of God, follow that way; and if another way appears, different from the first, and you quit the first and take the second, and the second works, it is all right. It would be nobler and better, however, to achieve rest and security through evenness, by which one might take God and enjoy him in any manner, in any thing, and not have to delay and hunt around for your special way: *that has been my joy!* To this end all kinds of activities may contribute and any work may be a help; but if it does not, let it go!

THE EXEMPLAR vol. II.*
By Henry Suso; trans. by Sr. Ann Edward

The distinctive feature about the German mystics of the fourteenth century is the enormous impulse they received from the writings of Meister Eckhart. This is especially true of his two chief disciples, the Dominicans Suso and Tauler. In Suso (1295-1365) Eckhartian theology is combined with the monastic tradition. The following is taken from Suso's Little Book of Eternal Wisdom.

THE EXEMPLAR vol. II.
How some men are drawn to God, unknown to themselves

"Hanc amavi et exquisivi a juventute mea, et quaesivi mihi sponsam assumere."

These words from the Book of Wisdom (8:2) spoken by the beautiful, lovable Eternal Wisdom, mean: "Her I loved and sought after from my youth; I sought to take her for my bride."

When he first concerned himself with temporal affairs, a restless soul strayed into the paths of irregularity. Then Eternal Wisdom met him in spiritual thoughts and drew him by means of sweetness and bitterness until she brought him to the right path of divine truth. Later, when reflecting on these marvelous attractions, he spoke to God: "Lovable, gentle Lord, since childhood my spirit has eagerly sought and thirsted for something which even now I do not fully understand. Lord, I have pursued this desire for many years without overtaking it because I do not really know what it is, even though it attracts my heart and soul to itself and its absence leaves me without true peace. At first, Lord, following the examples of my companions, I tried to find it in creatures, but the more I searched the less I found, and the closer I drew to it the further it receded from me, because before I could fully enjoy or abandon myself to any pleasure-yielding idea, an inner voice warned me: 'That is not what you are looking for.' This revulsion from all creatures has been my constant experience. Lord, even now my heart hungers for this unknown

*Henry Suso, O.P., *The Exemplar*, Vol. II (Chicago: The Priory Press, 1962), pp. 6-8, 46, 175-6. Out of print.

satisfaction and has often experienced what it is not; but what it is, that my heart has not yet discerned. Alas, cherished Lord of heaven, what is it, or why is it that this strange longing should make itself felt so mysteriously within me?"

Answer of Eternal Wisdom: Do you not recognize it? She has often embraced you lovingly and kept you from sinful ways until now she has attached you to herself alone.

The Servitor: Lord, I have never seen nor heard it; I do not know what it is.

Answer of Eternal Wisdom: That is the result of your intimacy with creatures and estrangement from her. But now open your eyes and see who I am. It is I, Eternal Wisdom, who have eternally singled you out for myself and embraced you with my unending providence. You would have been separated from me many times if, instead of supporting you on the way, I had forsaken you. Every creature was a source of disgust to you; this is a sure sign that you are one of my elect and that I want you for myself.

The Servitor: Lovable, gentle Wisdom, is it really you whom I have sought all these years? Are you the one for whom my soul has been pining? Alas, my God, why did you wait so long to show yourself to me? You surely delayed your coming. How many angry rivers I have had to wade.

Answer of Eternal Wisdom: If I had revealed myself sooner you would not have appreciated my kindness as keenly as you now do.

The Servitor: Ah, boundless Goodness, how tenderly you now prove your love for me. When I did not exist, you created me; when I abandoned you, you refused to leave me; when I tried to run away from you, you held me captive in love's chains. Ah, Eternal Wisdom, my heart now desires to burst open, to be shattered into a thousand pieces, to embrace you with constant love, and to consume all my days in perfect praise of you. Surely that man's happiness is flawless over whom you watch so lovingly and refuse any rest until it seeks all his rest in you alone. Alas, dear, lovable Wisdom, now that I have found the fulfillment of my soul's desires in you, despise not your poor creature but consider how insensible my heart is toward everything earthly, in joy and in sorrow. Lord, do you want my heart to repress its holy lovemaking? Permit, O Lord, permit my weary soul to whisper a few words with you, because my full heart can no longer keep its secret. There is no one in this wide world in whom my heart can confide except you, gentle, precious, beloved Lord and Brother. Lord, you alone see and understand the nature of an affectionate heart and realize that it is impossible for man to love what he does not know. Therefore, since I am obliged to love you alone, teach me to know you better so that I may love you in full measure.

Answer of Eternal Wisdom: According to the natural order, we follow the highest emanation of all beings from their first principle through the noblest beings down to the lowest, but the return to the first principle takes place through the lowest to the highest. Therefore, if you desire to gaze upon my uncreated divinity, you must first learn to know and love me in my suffering humanity, because that is the quickest way to eternal happiness.

The Servitor: In that case, Lord, I will remind you now of the immeasurable love which urged you to descend from your high throne, down from the kingly seat of the Father's heart, to thirty-three years of poverty and insult. By thus renouncing your eternal dignity, and especially by enduring a bitter and violent death, you proved your love for me and for all mankind. Lord, may the remembrance of these proofs of love constrain you to manifest yourself spiritually to my soul in the most lovable manner of which you are capable . . . .

Of heaven's boundless joy

Eternal Wisdom: Look heavenwards, and consider again where you belong. Heaven is your destination. Here you are a traveler, an exiled pilgrim. Therefore, the thought of loved ones waiting for you in heaven, preparing an affectionate welcome, getting ready for you an eternal place in the celestial household, should magnetize your spirit as the thought of friends and family awaiting his arrival makes an earthly traveler hasten his steps homeward. Remember also that you will derive much strength by reflecting that the saints yearn for you to join their ranks, desire to see you fight bravely and behave like a true knight in your encounters with the same adversities which they had to conquer, and that breathtaking joy is their eternal reward for having endured a few short years of temporal pain. Every drop of earthly bitterness will be changed into an ocean of heavenly sweetness.

The soul which was humbled on earth will in heaven be royally honored, and its every triumph over evil will be

A GREAT TREASURY OF CHRISTIAN SPIRITUALITY

recompensed and praised by my Father and all the heavenly host. This is a joy unknown to those who were not acquainted with earthly adversity. Brilliant jewels will glitter in the crown which was purchased at a high price. Glorious and shining will be the wounds and scars which were received for love of me. Believe me, in heaven you will have countless friends, and each one of them will love you more faithfully and tenderly than any father or mother loved an only child in this world.

How, after the example of Christ, a man should willingly resign himself to suffering

"I am as dark—but lovely, O daughter of Jerusalem—as the tents of Cedar" (Cant. 1:4).

Thus we read in the love book of the loving soul. The daughters of Jerusalem were surprised at the choice of a favorite wife by King Solomon. They could not understand why he chose as his favorite among so many women a negress.

What does the Holy Spirit mean by this? The black, beautiful negress who is more pleasing to God than all others, is a suffering person whom God exercises with great afflictions and adorns with patient abandonment.

Behold, daughter, it is easy to speak of suffering and to listen to others speak about it. But to actually experience it is very difficult.

It frequently happens that a suffering person is so oppressed that it seems to him that God has forgotten him, and he thinks to himself: "Alas, God, have you forgotten me? Do you not remember that I am still alive? What are your thoughts concerning me? How is it possible for your hand to be so severe, when your heart is so tender?"

God answers this loving complaint and says: "Behold the vast multitude of the saints, look at the lovely, living walls of the heavenly Jerusalem, and how the luminous stones of the city were cut and prepared with the knife of suffering. Now these stones glisten with bright lights. What were the experiences of St. Elizabeth? St. Paul was this world's scum. Job and Tobias were treated in like manner. St. Athanasius suffered so much that it seemed as if the whole world had decided to put him to death. Behold, all the saints suffered martyrdom, either of the heart or of the body!"

A suffering man should remember this and rejoice that God has deigned, by means of suffering, to associate him with his dearest friends. Therefore, let us endure mortification and martyrdom, starvation and humiliation, because great suffering will be followed by great reward.

Even though a man cannot remain constantly at peace in the midst of suffering, he does not lose God thereby—morning and evening are one day—as long as he does not become disobedient toward God.

If a suffering man's face becomes pale, if his mouth becomes parched, and his natural sweetness becomes bitter, let him look upward and say: "I am as dark . . . as the curtains of Salma" (Cant. 1:4). That is, the King suffering on the cross had lost the appearance of a man. Let the man who considers himself likened to the King by suffering, come forth. He says: "Ego sum vermis"—"I am a worm" (Ps. 21:7). Alas, thou Worm, brighter than the sun's rays, he who beholds you should not complain when he feels himself likened to you in suffering. He ought rather to incline his head for joy.

My child, when God assails you in this manner, you perhaps think that your sufferings are the greatest that any man endures. Do not think this. Every man is closest to himself. And I am no exception to this rule, because I often thought that my sufferings were extremely great. But we should let God be the judge.

I would not have written these things to you had not divine love moved me to do so. It seemed to me that in this way I was placing my shoulders under your burden and lightening it for you. When poor beggars meet they pass the time with each other and so forget their hunger for a little while. I would gladly have sent you the foot-towel which I took away from the dog and kept as a symbol. But it is so precious to me that I cannot part with it. Now take courage, suffer patiently, because hereafter you will have joy in the fair heavenly kingdom.

TAULER'S LIFE AND SERMONS*
trans. by S. Winkworth

John Tauler (1300-61), the other disciple of Eckhart and friend of Suso, was a natural born preacher and reformer. He taught a mystical form of personal religion based upon the conception of a "divine spark" or Godlike quality latent in every soul. This doctrine of the inner light was both orthodox and yet anticipates the Quaker position of the seventeenth century. The following is taken from one of Tauler's sermons and relates the states to self-fulfillment.

SERMON FOR THE FIRST SUNDAY AFTER EASTER
(From the Gospel for the day)
How we are to ascend by three stages to true peace and purity of heart.

John XX. 19—"Peace be to you."

"Peace be with you," said our beloved Lord to His disciples after His resurrection. All men by nature desire rest and peace, and are ever striving after it in all their manifold actions, efforts, and labours; and yet to all eternity they will never attain to true peace, unless they seek it where alone it is to be found,—in God. What, then, are the means and ways to find true peace, and the purest, highest, and most perfect truth? Now mark, I will speak unto you in a parable. As our blessed Lord drew His disciple St. John to Himself in a three-fold manner, even so does He now draw all who ever arrive at the deepest truth.

The first way in which our Lord drew St. John to Himself was when He called him out of the world and made him an Apostle. The second was when He suffered him to rest on His bosom; and the third and most perfect was on the holy day of Pentecost, when the Holy Ghost was given unto him, and a door was opened unto him through which he was taken up into heaven.

Thus, like St. John, is each man first called out of the world, when all his lower powers come to be governed by his highest reason, so that he learns to know himself and to exercise his free self-guiding power; so that he sets a watch over his words,

*Reprinted from John Tauler, *Life and Sermons*. London: Allenson and Co., 1962, with the permission of James Clarke and Co., Ltd., London, pp. 315-319.

saying nothing to anyone which he would not wish to be said to himself;—over his impulses, marking whether they proceed from God and tend towards Him;—over his thoughts, that he does not voluntarily indulge in any evil or vain imaginations, or that, if such suggest themselves, they should be made only an incentive and stepping-stone to better things;—over his works, that in his undertakings he may have a single eye to the glory of God and the welfare of mankind. In this wise does the Lord call thee out of the world, and make thee an apostle of Christ to thy fellow-man, and so thou learnest to convert the outward into the inward man, which is the first step in the Christian course.

Secondly; wilt thou with St. John rest on the loving heart of our Lord Jesus Christ, thou must be transformed into the beauteous image of our Lord by a constant, earnest contemplation thereof, considering His holy meekness and humility, the deep, fiery love that He bore to His friends and His foes, and His mighty, obedient resignation which He manifested in all the paths wherein His Father called Him to tread. Next call to mind the boundless charity which He showed to all men, and also His blessed poverty. Heaven and earth were His, and He called them not His own. In all His words and deeds, He looked only to the glory of His Father and the salvation of mankind. And now ye must gaze much more closely and deeply into the glorious image of our Lord Jesus Christ than I can show you with my outward teaching, and maintain a continual, earnest effort and aspiration after it. Then look attentively at thyself, how unlike thou art to this image, and behold thy own littleness. Here will thy Lord let thee rest on Him. There is no better and more profitable way to this end while in our present state, than to receive worthily the sacrament of the body of Christ, and to follow the counsel of one on whom the light of grace has shone more brightly than it has on thee. In the glorious likeness of Christ thou wilt be made rich, and find all the solace and sweetness in the world.

But there are many who, having advanced thus far, think in their haste that they have conquered for their own the ground on which they stand, while yet they are far from the goal. Although St. John had lain on Christ's bosom, yet he let his cloak fall and fled when the Jews laid hands on Christ. Therefore, however holy may be thy walk in these two paths, look to it that, if thou art assailed, thou do not let thy mantle fall through thy hasty thought for thyself. It is good and holy that thou shouldst exercise thyself in these two ways, and let no creature turn thee aside therefrom, until God Himself draws thee up into a closer union with Himself. If He thus draw thee up, then let go all forms and images, and suffer Him to work as with His instrument. It is more well-pleasing to Him, and more profitable to thee, that thou shouldst leave Him to do as He will in thee for a moment, than that thou shouldst exercise thyself in lower things for a hundred years. Now some may ask: Art thou not yet got beyond all this? I answer: No; beyond the image of our Lord Jesus Christ may no man come. Thou shouldst ask: Art thou not got beyond the ways and works that thou hast called thine own? Look to it diligently and be quick to perceive the commands of God, and let each good work be followed by another.

In the third place, when the Holy Spirit was given to St. John, then was the door of heaven opened unto him. This happens to some with a convulsion of the mind, to others calmly and gradually. In it are fulfilled those words of St. Paul: "Eye hath not seen, nor ear heard, nor hath it entered into the heart of man to conceive the things which God hath prepared for them that love Him; but God hath revealed them unto us by His spirit." Let no man boast that he is continually drawing nearer to the highest perfection possible while here on earth, unless the outward man have been converted into the inward man; then, indeed, it is possible for him to be received up on high, and to behold the wonders and riches of God. Believe me, children, one who would know much about these high matters, would often have to keep his bed, for his bodily frame could not support it. Further, know ye that before that can come to pass, of which we have here been speaking, nature must endure many a death, outward and inward. But to such death, eternal life answers. Children, this is not the work of a day or a year. Be not discouraged; it takes time, and requires simplicity, purity, and self-surrender, and these virtues are the shortest road to it. Through such exercises as we have described, a man obtains true purity of mind and body, such as St. John possessed in a high and peculiar manner; what our Lord meant when he said: "Blessed are the pure in heart, for they shall see God." A pure heart is more precious in the sight of God than aught else on earth. A pure heart is a fair, fitly-adorned chamber, the dwelling of the Holy Ghost, a golden temple of the Godhead; a sanctuary of the only-begotten Son, in which He worships the Heavenly Father; an altar of the grand, divine sacrifice, on which the Son is daily offered to the Heavenly Father. A pure heart is the throne of the Supreme Judge; the seat and secret chamber of the Holy Trinity; a lamp bearing the Eternal Light; a secret council-chamber of the Divine Persons; a treasury of divine riches; a storehouse of divine sweetness; a panoply of eternal wisdom; a cell of divine solitude; the reward of all the life and sufferings of Christ. A pure heart is a tabernacle of the Holy Father; a bride of Christ; a friend of the Holy Ghost; a delight to the eyes of all saints; a sister of the angels; a cause of joy to the heavenly hosts; a brother of all good men; a terror to the Devil; a victory and conquest over all temptation; a weapon against all assaults; a reservoir of divine benefits; a treasury of all virtue; an example to all men; a restoration of all that has ever been lost. Now, what is a pure heart? It is, as we have said before, a heart which finds its whole and only satisfaction in God, which relishes and desires nothing but God, whose thoughts and intents are ever occupied with God, to which all that is not of God is strange and jarring, which keeps itself as far as possible apart from all unworthy images, joys, and griefs, and all outward cares and anxieties, and makes all these work together for good; for to the pure all things are pure, and to the gentle is nothing bitter. Amen!

FROM GLORY TO GLORY*

By Gregory of Nyssa; trans. by Herbert Musurillo

*St. Gregory of Nyssa, (4th century), is at once the most
important and the most neglected of the early Christian
mystical theologians. He was Bishop of Nyssa in Asia Minor
during the great Arian controversy. His mystical and ascetical
works have always been well-known in the Oriental Church.
Only in our own day have they been rediscovered by the West.
The following is taken from Gregory's commentary on the
Canticle of Canticles.*

FROM GLORY TO GLORY
The Myrrh of Penance (ibid., sermon 12, 1016C-1024B)

*I rose up to open my beloved; my hands dropped with myrrh,
and my fingers were full of myrrh* (Cant. 5-5). It is impossible
for the living Word to be present in us—I mean that pure,
invisible Spouse Who unites the soul to Himself by sanctity
and incorruptibility—unless by the mortification of our bodies
on earth we tear away the veil of the flesh, and in this way open
the door to the Word that He may come and dwell with the soul.
This is clear from the divine instruction of the Apostle as well
as from the words just spoken by the bride. *I rose up,* she says
to open to my beloved, and this I did by making my hands
fountains of myrrh which flowed with spices, and showing
that myrrh has filled my fingers. And by her words she shows
us how she opened the door to her Spouse: Being buried with
Him unto death by Baptism, I rose again. For the resurrection
would have accomplished nothing had it not been preceded by
a voluntary death. Now an indication that it was voluntary is
the drop of myrrh that flows from her hands, and the fact that
her fingers too are filled with this aromatic spice. For she says
that the myrrh did not come to her hand from any other source;
for otherwise one might have thought that the symbol of the
myrrh referred to something purely accidental and
indeliberate. But she tells us that her hands flowed with myrrh
of their own accord (and the hands symbolize the effective
operations of the soul); that is, there was a free and

*Reprinted by permission of Charles Scribner's sons from *From Glory to Glory*. Texts
from Gregory of Nyssa's Mystical Writings, translated and edited by Herbert Musurillo,
S.J., 1961, pp. 254-255.

spontaneous mortification of all her bodily passions, and this is why it is said that it filled all her fingers. For the text uses the word "fingers" to suggest all the different sorts of activity connected with the practice of virtue. Hence the complete meaning of the text is as follows: I received the power of resurrection by mortifying my members on earth; this mortification I undertook willingly; the myrrh was not put into my hands by someone else, but flowed from my own free will. Thus the same disposition of soul may be sent constantly in all my works of virtue, which the text calls "fingers."

Among those who practice virtue, you may see some who have died to one passion, but are alive to others. So, for example, we see men who have mortified incontinence, but still cultivate pride inclination that disfigures the soul, such as avarice, anger, ambition, love of honor, and the like. And if any of these are still alive in the soul, one cannot show one's fingers as *full of myrrh*. For the mortification and removal of sin has not extended to all our life. But when all the fingers have been filled with myrrh in this way, then the soul rises up and opens to the Spouse.

Hence it would seem that the great Paul has rightly understood the words of his Master, unless the grain be dissolved by death the sheaf cannot grow. This is the doctrine that he preaches to the Church: that death must precede life, and that it is impossible for life to be in a man unless it enter by way of death.

THE SCALE OF PERFECTION*
By Walter Hilton

Hilton has already been introduced in the preceding chapter. He is one of the few mystics who give advice on the whole road of spirituality. Thus his practical parable in this selection is classic. He likens a physical pilgrimage to Jerusalem to the spiritual journey of discovering God.

THE SCALE OF PERFECTION
How one who wishes to reach Jerusalem, the city of peace, which represents contemplation, must have faith, be very humble, and endure troubles of body and soul

Since you wish to learn some way by which you can approach this reformation, if the Lord Jesus gives me grace I will tell you what I consider the shortest and simplest way. To explain it, I will use the simile of a good pilgrim.

A man once wished to go to Jerusalem, and since he did not know the way, he called on another man who, he hoped, knew the way, and asked him for information. This other man told him that he would not reach it without great hardship and effort. 'The way is long,' he said, 'and there is great danger from thieves and bandits, as well as many other difficulties which beset a man on this journey. Furthermore, there are many different roads which seem to lead towards it, but every day men are killed and robbed, and never reach their goal. But I can guarantee one road which will lead you to the city of Jerusalem if you will keep to it. On this road your life will be safe, but you will have to undergo robbery, violence, and great distress.'

The pilgrim replied: 'I do not mind how much hardship I have to undergo on the road, so long as my life is spared and I reach my destination. So tell me all you know, and I faithfully promise to follow your instructions.' The other answered, 'I will set you on the right road. See that you carry out my instructions. Do not allow anything that you may see, hear, or feel on the road to delay you. Do not stop for it, look at it, take pleasure in it, or fear it. Keep on your way without halting, and

---

*Reprinted from *The Scale of Perfection* by Walter Hilton. © Geoffrey Chapman Publishers, 1975, with the permission of Abbey Press, St. Meinrad, Indiana, pp. 71-74.

remember that your goal is Jerusalem; that is what you want, and nothing else. If you are robbed, beaten, insulted, and treated with contempt, do not retaliate if you value your life. Resign yourself to such injuries and disregard them, lest you suffer worse things. And if people delay you with foolish tales and lies in order to distract you and make you abandon your pilgrimage, turn a deaf ear to them and make no reply save that you wish to reach Jerusalem. And if people offer you gifts or provide opportunities for you to enrich yourself, disregard them; keep your mind constantly on Jerusalem. If you will keep to this road and do as I have said, I guarantee that you will not be killed, and that you will arrive at the place for which you long.'

Spiritually interpreted, Jerusalem is the vision of peace, and symbolizes contemplation in the perfect love of God. For contemplation is nothing other than the vision of Jesus, who is our true peace. Therefore if you really desire to attain this blessed vision of true peace and to be a true pilgrim to Jerusalem, I will set you on the right road as far as I can, although I have never been there myself. The beginning of this high road that you must travel is reformation in faith, which, as I have already said, is grounded in humility, faith, and the laws of the Church. And if you have been reformed by the sacrament of penance according to the laws of Holy Church, you can rest assured that, despite your earlier sins, you are on the right road. If you wish to make swift and substantial progress along this road, you must constantly bear in mind two things, humility and love. That is, I am nothing, and I want only one thing. Fix the true meaning of these words permanently in your subconscious mind and purpose, so that they will guide you even when you are not thinking of them. Humility says, 'I am nothing, I have nothing.' Love says, 'I desire one thing only, which is Jesus.' When deftly touched by the finger of reason, these two strings, secured by the thought of Jesus, make sweet harmony in the harp of the soul, for the lower you strike on one, the higher the sound on the other. Under the influence of humility, the less you feel that you are or possess, the greater will be your love and longing for Jesus. I am not speaking merely of the kind of humility that a soul feels at the sight of its own sin or weakness, or of the sorrows of this life, or when it sees the better lives of other Christians; for although this kind of humility is sound and wholesome, it is still of an elementary and worldly type, not pure, gentle, and perfect. I am speaking rather of the humility that a soul feels by grace as it contemplates the infinite being and wondrous goodness of Jesus. And if you cannot yet see this with the eyes of the soul, do believe in its reality. For having once caught a glimpse of his being, whether by true faith or by spiritual experience, you will see yourself not only as the most wretched of men but as worthless, even though you had never sinned. This is perfect humility, for in comparison to Jesus, who is all, you are nothing. You should also realize that you possess nothing, like a vessel that stands empty, incapable of filling itself; for however many good works you perform, spiritual or bodily, you have nothing until you feel the love of Jesus within you. It is this precious liquor alone that can fill your soul, and no other. And since this alone is so precious and noble, you must realize that whatever you may have or achieve is of no value or satisfaction without the love of Jesus. Put everything else behind you and forget it; only then can you have what is best of all.

A real pilgrim going to Jerusalem leaves his house and land, wife and children; he divests himself of all that he possesses in order to travel light and without encumbrances. Similarly, if you wish to be a spiritual pilgrim you must divest yourself of all that you possess; that is, both of good deeds and bad, and leave them all behind you. Recognize your own poverty, so that you will not place any confidence in your own work; instead, be always desiring the grace of deeper love, and seeking the spiritual presence of Jesus. If you do this, you will be setting your heart wholly on reaching Jerusalem, and on nothing else. In other words, set your heart wholly on obtaining the love of Jesus and whatever spiritual vision of himself that he is willing to grant, for it is to this end alone that you have been created and redeemed; this is your beginning and your end, your joy and your bliss. Therefore, whatever you may possess, and however fruitful your activities, regard them all as worthless without the inward certainty and experience of this love. Keep this intention constantly in mind and hold to it firmly; it will sustain you among all the perils of your pilgrimage. It will protect you from thieves and robbers—that is, from evil spirits—for although they may rob and assault you with different temptations, your life will always be safe. In short, do as I tell you, and you will escape out of all dangers and arrive speedily at the city of Jerusalem.

Now that you are on the road and know your proper destination, you must begin your journey. The departure consists entirely of spiritual—and when necessary, bodily—activity, and you must direct this activity wisely in the following way. I regard any activity that you undertake as excellent provided that it suits your particular calling and conditions of life, and that it fosters this high desire for the love of Jesus, and makes it more sincere, more comforting, and more productive of all virtues. It may be prayer, meditation, reading, or working, but so long as the activity is one which deepens the love of Jesus in your heart and will, and withdraws your thoughts and affections from worldly trivialities, it is good. But should it grow stale and lose its value, and you consider that some other activity would be more beneficial and bring greater grace with it, then adopt it and abandon the earlier one. For although the desire and longing of your heart for Jesus should be constant and unchanging, you are at liberty to vary your spiritual exercises in order to stimulate this desire, and they may well be changed when you feel that grace moves you to do so.

The relation of spiritual activities to desire is similar to that of sticks to a fire. For the more sticks are laid on the fire, the greater is the fire: similarly, the more varying spiritual exercises that a man performs to stimulate his desire for God, the stronger and more ardent it will be. Therefore, if you are free and are not bound by any particular obligation, consider carefully which activity is best suited to you, and which most fosters your desire for Jesus, and undertake it. Do not deliberately bind yourself to an unchangeable routine which would prevent your heart loving Jesus freely should you receive a special visitation of grace. For I will tell you which activities are always good and essential. Any custom is good provided that it tends to foster virtue and prevent sin. Such a custom should never be abandoned, for you must always try to cultivate humility, patience, temperance, purity, and all other virtues. But any custom that prevents the adoption of a better should be abandoned as soon as time and circumstances permit. For instance, if someone is accustomed to recite a certain number or rosaries, or meditate in a certain way for a fixed time, or watch, or kneel for a set time, or observe any other outward custom, such customs should sometimes be set aside when there is reasonable cause, or if greater grace is given by other means.

THE RELEASE OF THE SPIRIT*
By Watchman Nee

Watchman Nee is a twentieth century Chinese evangelical Protestant witness to the spiritual life. His life was spent in preaching and writing. He was imprisoned in 1952 by the Chinese communists and died in prison twenty years later. Many of his writings were smuggled out of prison by guards whom he had converted. His writings are currently quite popular among prayer groups today.

THE IMPORTANCE OF BROKENNESS

Anyone who serves God will discover sooner or later that the great hindrance to his work is not others but himself. He will discover that his outward man and his inward man are not in harmony, for both are tending toward opposite directions. He will also sense the inability of his outward man to submit to the spirit's control, thus rendering him incapable of obeying God's highest commands. He will quickly detect that the greatest difficulty lies in his outward man, for it hinders him from using his spirit.

Many of God's servants are not able to do even the most elementary works. Ordinarily they should be enabled by the exercise of their spirit to know God's word, to discern the spiritual condition of another, to send forth God's messages under anointing and to receive God's revelations. Yet due to the distractions of the outward man, their spirit does not seem to function properly. It is basically because their outward man has never been dealt with. For this reason revival, zeal, pleading and activity are but a waste of time. As we shall see, there is just one basic dealing which can enable man to be useful before God: brokenness.

The Inward Man and the Outward Man

Notice how the Bible divides man into two parts: "For I delight in the law of God according to the inward man" (Rom. 7:22). Our inward man delights in the Law of God. ". . . To be strengthened with power by his Spirit in the inner man" (Eph.

* © 1965 by Sure Foundation, Rt. 2, Box 74, Cloverdale, Ind. Reprinted with permission, pp. 9-18.

3:16), and Paul also tells us, "But if indeed our outward man is consumed, yet the inward is renewed day by day" (2 Cor. 4:16).

When God comes to indwell us by His Spirit, life and power, He comes into our spirit which we are calling the inward man. Outside of this inward man is the soul wherein function our thoughts, emotions and will. The outermost man is our physical body. Thus we will speak of the inward man as the spirit, the outer man as the soul and the outermost man as the body. We must never forget that our inward man is the human spirit where God dwells, where His Spirit mingles with our spirit. Just as we are dressed in clothes, so our inward man "wears" an outward man: the spirit "wears" the soul. And similarly, the spirit and soul "wear" the body. It is quite evident that men are generally more conscious of the outer and outermost man, and they hardly recognize or understand their spirit at all.

We must know that he who can work for God is the one whose inward man can be released. The basic difficulty of a servant of God lies in the failure of the inward man to break through the outward man. Therefore we must recognize before God that the first difficulty to our work is not in others but in ourselves. Our spirit seems to be wrapped in a covering so that it cannot easily break forth. If we have never learned how to release our inward man by breaking through the outward man, we are not able to serve. Nothing can so hinder us as this outward man. Whether our works are fruitful or not depends upon whether our outward man has been broken by the Lord so that the inward man can pass through that brokenness and come forth. This is the basic problem. The Lord wants to break our outward man in order that the inward man may have a way out. When the inward man is released, both unbelievers and Christians will be blessed.

Nature Has Its Way of Breaking

The Lord Jesus tells us in John 12, "Except the grain of wheat falling into the ground die, it abides alone; but if it die, it bears much fruit." Life is in the grain of wheat, but there is a shell, a very hard shell on the outside. As long as that shell is not split open, the wheat cannot sprout and grow. "Except the grain of wheat falling into the ground die . . . ." What is this death? It is the cracking open of the shell through the working together of temperature, humidity, in the soil. Once the shell is split open, the wheat begins to grow. So the question here is not whether there is life within, but whether the outside shell is cracked open.

The Scripture continues by saying, "He that loves his life (Greek, *soul)* shall lose it, and he that hates his life (Greek, *soul)* in this world shall keep it to life eternal" (v. 25). The Lord shows us here that the outer shell is our own life (our soul life), while the life within is the eternal life which He has given to us. To allow the inner life to come forth, it is imperative that the outward life be replaced. Should the outward remain unbroken, the inward would never be able to come forth.

It is necessary (in this writing) that we direct these words to that group of people who have the Lord's life. Among those who possess the life of the Lord can be found two distinct conditions: one includes those in whom life is confined, restricted, imprisoned and unable to come forth; the other includes those in whom the Lord has forged a way, and life is thus released from them.

The question thus is not how to obtain life, but rather how to allow this life to come forth. When we say we need the Lord to break us, this is not merely a way of speaking, nor is it only a doctrine. It is vital that we be broken by the Lord. It is not that the life of the Lord cannot cover the earth, but rather that His life is imprisoned by us. It is not that the Lord cannot bless the church, but that the Lord's life is so confined within us that there is no flowing forth. If the outward man remains unbroken, we can never be a blessing to His church, and we cannot expect the word of God to be blessed by Him through us!

The Alabaster Box Must Be Broken

The Bible tells of the pure spikenard. God purposely used this term "pure" in His word to show that it is truly spiritual. But if the alabaster box is not broken, the pure spikenard will not flow forth. Strange to say, many are still treasuring the alabaster box, thinking that its value exceeds that of the ointment. Many think that their outward man is more precious than their inward man. This becomes the problem in the church. One will treasure his cleverness, thinking he is quite important; another will treasure his own emotions, esteeming himself as an important person; others highly regard themselves, feeling they are better than others, their eloquence surpasses that of others, their quickness of action and exactness of judgment are superior, and so forth. However, we are not antique collectors; we are not vase admirers; we are those who desire to smell only the fragrance of the ointment. Without the breaking of the outward, the inward will not come forth. Thus individually we have no flowing out, but also the church does not have a living way. Why then should we hold ourselves as so precious, if our outward contains instead of releases the fragrance?

The Holy Spirit has not ceased working. One event after another, one thing after another, comes to us. Each disciplinary working of the Holy Spirit has but one purpose: to break our outward man so that our inward man may come through. Yet here is our difficulty: we fret over trifles, we murmur at small losses. The Lord is preparing a way to use us, yet scarcely has His hand touched us when we feel unhappy, even to the extent of quarreling with God and becoming negative in our attitude. Since being saved, we have been touched many times in various ways by the Lord, all with the purpose of breaking our outward man. Whether we are conscious of it or not, the aim of the Lord is to break this outward man.

So the Treasure is in the earthen vessel, but if the earthen vessel is not broken, who can see the Treasure within? What is the final objective of the Lord's working in our lives? It is to break this earthen vessel, to break our alabaster box, to crack open our shell. The Lord longs to find a way to bless the world through those who belong to Him. Brokenness is the way of blessing, the way of fragrance, the way of fruitfulness, but it is also a path sprinkled with blood. Yes, there is blood from many wounds. When we offer ourselves to the Lord to be at His service, we cannot afford to be lenient, to spare ourselves. We must allow the Lord utterly to crack our outward man, so that He may find a way for His out-working.

Each of us must find out for himself what is the mind of the Lord in his life. It is a most lamentable fact that many do not know what is the mind or intention of the Lord for their lives. How much they need for Him to open their eyes, to see that everything which comes into their lives can be meaningful. The Lord has not wasted even one thing. To understand the Lord's purpose, is to see very clearly that He is aiming at a single objective: the breaking of the outward man.

However, too many, even before the Lord raises a hand, are already upset. Oh, we must realize that all the experiences, troubles and trials which the Lord sends us are for our highest good. We cannot expect the Lord to give better things, for these are His best. Should one approach the Lord and pray, saying, "O Lord, please let me choose the best," I believe He would tell him, "What I have given you is the best; your daily trials are for your greatest profit." So the motive behind all the orderings of God is to break our outward man. Once this occurs and our spirit can come forth, we begin to be able to exercise our spirit.

The Timing in Our Brokenness

The Lord employs two different ways to break our outward man; one is gradual, the other sudden. To some, the Lord gives a sudden breaking followed by a gradual one. With others, the Lord arranges that they have constant daily trials, until one day He brings about large-scale breaking. If it is not the sudden first and then the gradual, then it is the gradual followed by the sudden. It would seem the Lord usually spends several years upon us before He can accomplish this work of breaking.

The timing is in His hand. We cannot shorten the time, though we certainly can prolong it. In some lives the Lord is able to accomplish this work after a few years of dealing; in others it is evident that after ten or twenty years the work is still unfinished. This is most serious! Nothing is more grievous than wasting God's time. How often the church is hindered! We can preach by using our mind, we can stir others by using our emotions; yet if we do not know how to use our spirit, the Spirit of God cannot touch people through us. The loss is great, should we needlessly prolong the time.

Therefore, if we have never before wholly and intelligently consecrated ourselves to the Lord, let us do so now, saying: "Lord, for the future of the church, for the future of the gospel, for Thy way, and also for my own life, I offer myself without condition, without reservation, into Thy hands. Lord, I delight to offer myself unto Thee and am willing to let Thee have Thy full way through me."

The Meaning of the Cross

Often we hear about the cross. Perhaps we are too familiar with the term. But what is the cross after all? When we really understand the cross we shall see it means the breaking of the outward man. The cross reduces the outward man to death; it splits open the human shell. The cross must break all that belongs to our outward man—our opinions, our ways, our cleverness, our self-love, our all. The way is clear, in fact crystal clear.

As soon as our outward man is destroyed, our spirit can easily come forth. Consider a brother as an example. All who know him acknowledge that he has a keen mind, a forceful will, and deep emotions. But instead of being impressed by these natural characteristics of his soul, they realize they have met his spirit. Whenever people are fellowshipping with him, they encounter a spirit, a clean spirit. Why? Because all that is of his soul has been destroyed.

Take as another example, a sister. Those who know her recognize that she is of a quick disposition—quick in thought, quick of speech, quick to confess, quick in writing letters, and quick to tear up what she has written. However, those who meet her do not meet her quickness but rather her spirit. She is one who has been utterly destroyed and has become transparent. This destruction of the outward man is such a basic matter. We should not cling to our weak, soulish characteristics, still emitting the same fragrance even after five or ten years of the Lord's dealing with us. No, we must allow the Lord to forge a way in our lives.

Two Reasons for Not Being Broken

Why is it that after many years of dealing some remain the same? Some individuals have a forceful will; some have strong emotions; and others have a strong mind. Since the Lord is able to break these, why is it that after many years some are still unchanged? We believe there are two main reasons.

First, many who live in darkness are not seeing the hand of God. While God is working, while God is destroying, they do not recognize it as being from Him. They are devoid of light, seeing only men opposing them. They imagine their environment is just too difficult, that circumstances are to blame. So they continue in darkness and despair.

May God give us a revelation to see what is from His hand, that we may kneel down and say to him, "It is Thou; since it is Thou, I will accept." At least we must recognize *whose* hand it is that deals with us. It is not a human hand, nor our family's, not the brothers' and sisters' in the church, but God's. We need to learn how to kneel down and kiss the hand, love the hand that deals with us, even as Madame Guyon did. We must have this light to see that whatever the Lord has done, we accept and believe; the Lord can do no wrong.

Second, another great hindrance to the work of breaking the outer man is self-love. We must ask God to take away the heart of self-love. As He deals with us in response to our prayer, we should worship and say, "O Lord, if this be Thy hand, let me accept it from my heart." Let us remember that the one reason for all misunderstanding, all fretfulness, all discontent, is that we secretly love ourselves. Thus we plan a way whereby we can deliver ourselves. Many times problems arise due to our seeking a way of escape—an escape from the working of the cross.

He who has ascended the cross and refuses to drink the vinegar mingled with gall is the one who knows the Lord. Many go up to the cross rather reluctantly, still thinking of drinking vinegar mingled with gall to alleviate their pains. All who say, "The cup which the Father has given me, shall I not drink it?" will not drink the cup of vinegar mingled with gall. They can only drink of one cup, not two. Such as these are without any self-love. Self-love is a basic difficulty. May the Lord speak to us today that we may be able to pray: "O my God, I have seen that all things come from Thee. All my ways these five years, ten years, or twenty years, are of Thee. Thou hast so worked to attain Thy purpose, which is none other than that Thy life may be lived out through me. But I have been foolish. I did not see. I did many things to deliver myself, thus delaying Thy time. Today I see Thy hand. I am willing to offer myself to Thee. Once again I place myself in Thy hands."

Expect to See Wounds

There is no one more beautiful than one who is broken! Stubbornness and self-love give way to beauty in one who has been broken by God. We see Jacob in the Old Testament, how even in his mother's womb he struggled with his brother. He was subtle, tricky, deceitful. Yet his life was full of sorrows and grief. When a youth, he fled from home. For twenty years he was cheated by Laban. The wife of his heart's love, Rachel, died prematurely. The son of his love, Joseph, was sold. Years later Benjamin was detained in Egypt. He was successively dealt with by God, meeting misfortune after misfortune. He was stricken by God once, twice; indeed, his whole history could be said to be a history of being stricken by God. Finally after many such dealings, the man Jacob was transformed. In his last few years, he was quite transparent. How dignified was his answer to Pharaoh! How beautiful was his end, when he worshipped God on his staff! How clear were his blessings to his descendants! After reading the last page of his history, we want to bow our heads and worship God. Here is one who is matured, who knows God. Several decades of dealings have resulted in Jacob's outward man being broken. In his old age, the picture is a beautiful one.

Each of us has much of the same Jacob nature in us. Our only hope is that the Lord may blaze a way out, breaking the outward man to such a degree that the inward man may come out and be seen. This is precious, and this is the way of those who serve the Lord. Only thus can we serve; only thus can we lead men to the Lord. All else is limited in its value. Doctrine does not have much use nor does theology. What is the use of mere mental knowledge of the Bible if the outward man remains unbroken? Only the person through whom God can come forth is useful.

After our outward man has been stricken, dealt with, and led through various trials, we have wounds upon us, thus allowing the spirit to emerge. We are afraid to meet some brothers and sisters whose whole being remains intact, never having been dealt with and changed. May God have mercy upon us in showing us clearly this way and in revealing to us that it is the only way. May He also show us that herein is seen the purpose of all His dealings with us in these few years, say ten or twenty. Thus let no one despise the Lord's dealings. May He truly reveal to us what is meant by the breaking of the outward man. Should the outward man remain whole, everything would be merely in our mind, utterly useless. Let us expect the Lord to deal with us thoroughly.

INTERIOR CASTLE*
By St. Teresa of Avila

St. Teresa is the only author carried through all these chapters. Perhaps of all the mystics she is the most easily understood and has experienced all of the degrees of the spiritual life. Herein lies her account of her first mystical experience. The touchstone of the experience is the certainty that God has been in one and one has been in God.

INTERIOR CASTLE
Begins to explain how in prayer the soul is united with God. Describes how we may know that we are not mistaken about this.

Oh, sisters! How shall I ever be able to tell you of the riches and the treasures and the delights which are to be found in the fifth Mansions? I think it would be better if I were to say nothing of the Mansions I have not yet treated, for no one can describe them, the understanding is unable to comprehend them and no comparisons will avail to explain them, for earthly things are quite insufficient for this purpose. Send me light from Heaven, my Lord, that I may enlighten these Thy servants, to some of whom Thou are often pleased to grant fruition of these joys, lest, when the devil transfigures himself into an angel of light, he should deceive them, for all their desires are occupied in desiring to please Thee.

Although I said "to some," there are really very few who do not enter these Mansions that I am about to describe. Some get farther than others; but, as I say, the majority manage to get inside. Some of the things which are in this room and which I will mention here, are, I am sure, attained by very few;[37] but, if they do no more than reach the door, God is showing them great mercy by granting them this; for, though many are called, few are chosen.[38] So I must say here that, though all of us who wear this sacred habit of Carmel are[39] called to prayer

---

*Reprinted from *The Interior Castle* in *The Complete Works of St. Teresa,* trans. and edited by E. Allison Peers from the critical edition of P. Silverio De Santa Teresa, O.C.D., published in three volumes by Sheed and Ward, Inc., New York. Excerpt from Image Books, 1961, pp. 96-107.

37. Gracian has scored through part of this sentence in the autograph.
38. St. Matthew xx, 16.
39. Gracian substitutes for "are": "follow the rule of being."

and contemplation—because that was the first principle of our Order and because we are descendent upon the line of those holy Fathers of ours from Mount Carmel who sought this treasure, this precious pearl of which we speak, in such great solitude and with such contempt for the world—few of us[40] prepare ourselves for the Lord to reveal it to us. As far as externals are concerned, we are on the right road to attaining the essential virtues; but we shall need to do a very great deal before we can attain to this higher state and we must on no account be careless. So let us pause here, my sisters, and beg the Lord that, since to some extent it is possible for us to enjoy Heaven upon earth, He will grant us His help so that it will not be our fault if we miss anything; may He also show us the road and give strength to our souls so that we may dig until we find this hidden treasure, since it is quite true that we have it within ourselves. This I should like to explain if the Lord is pleased to give me the knowledge.

I said "strength to our souls," because you must understand that we do not need bodily strength if God our Lord does not give it us; there is no one for whom He makes it impossible to buy His riches; provided each gives what he has, He is content. Blessed be so great a God! But observe, daughters, that, if you are to gain this, He would have you keep back nothing; whether it be little or much, He will have it all for Himself, and according to what you know yourself to have given, the favours He will grant you will be small or great. There is no better test than this of whether or no our prayer attains to union. Do not think it is a state, like the last, in which we dream; I say "dream," because the soul seems to be, as it were, drowsy, so that it neither seems asleep nor feels awake. Here we are all asleep, and fast asleep, to the things of the world, and to ourselves (in fact, for the short time that the condition lasts, the soul is without consciousness and has no power to think, even though it may desire to do so). There is no need now for it to devise any method of suspending the thought. Even in loving, if it is able to love, it cannot understand how or what it is that it loves, nor what it would desire; in fact, it has completely died to the world so that it may live more fully in God. This is a delectable death, a snatching of the soul from all the activities which it can perform while it is in the body; a death full of delight, for, in order to come closer to God, the soul appears to

40. Gracian inserts the word "perhaps."

have withdrawn so far from the body that I do not know if it has still life enough to be able to breathe.[41] I have just been thinking about this and I believe it has not; or at least, if it still breathes, it does so without realizing it. The mind would like to occupy itself wholly in understanding something of what it feels, and, as it has not the strength to do this, it becomes so dumbfounded that, even if any consciousness remains to it, neither hands nor feet can move; as we commonly say of a person who has fallen into a swoon, it might be taken for dead. Oh, the secrets of God! I should never weary of trying to describe them to you, if I thought I could do so successfully. I do not mind if I write any amount of nonsense, provided that just once in a way I can write sense, so that we may give great praise to the Lord.

I said that there was no question here of dreaming, whereas in the Mansion that I have just described the soul is doubtful as to what has really happened until it has had a good deal of experience of it. It wonders if the whole thing was imagination, if it has been asleep, if the favour was a gift of God, or if the devil was transfigured into an angel of light. It retains a thousand suspicions, and it is well that it should, for, as I said, we can sometimes be deceived in this respect, even by our own nature. For, although there is less opportunity for the poisonous creatures to enter, a few little lizards, being very agile, can hide themselves all over the place; and, although they do no harm—especially, as I said, if we take no notice of them—they correspond to the little thoughts which proceed from the imagination and from what has been said it will be seen that they are often very troublesome. Agile though they are, however, the lizards cannot enter this Mansion, for neither imagination nor memory nor understanding can be an obstacle to the blessings that are bestowed in it. And I shall venture to affirm that, if this is indeed union with God,[42] the devil cannot enter or do any harm; for His Majesty is in such close contact and union with the essence of the soul[43] that he will not dare to approach, nor can he even understand this secret thing. That much is evident: for it is said that he does not

41. Luis de Leon modifies this passage [which has been slightly paraphrased in translation, the construction in the Spanish being rather obscure], reading, after "delight": "for, although it [the soul] is in Him, according to the truth, it appears to have withdrawn so far from the body, in order to come closer to God, that I do not know, etc."
42. "Of the soul alone," inserts Gracian, interlineally.
43. Gracian deletes "the essence of."

understand our thoughts;[44] still less, therefore, will he understand a thing so secret that God will not even entrust our thoughts with it.[45] Oh, what a great blessing is this state in which that accursed one can do us no harm! Great are the gains which come to the soul with God working in it and neither we ourselves nor anyone else hindering Him. What will He not give Who so much loves giving and can give all that He will?

I fear I may be leaving you confused by saying "if this is indeed union with God" and suggesting that there are other kinds of union. But of course there are! If we are really very fond of vanities the devil will send us into transports over them; but these are not like the transports of God, nor is there the same delight and satisfaction for the soul or the same peace and joy. That joy is greater than all the joys of earth, and greater than all its delights, and all its satisfactions, so that there is no evidence that these satisfactions and those of the earth have a common origin; and they are apprehended, too, very differently, as you will have learned by experience. I said once[46] that it is as if the one kind had to do with the grosser part of the body, and the other kind penetrated to the very marrow of the bones; that puts it well, and I know no better way of expressing it.

But I fancy that even now you will not be satisfied, for you will think that you may be mistaken, and that these interior matters are difficult to investigate. In reality, what has been said will be sufficient for anyone who has experienced this blessing, for there is a great difference between the false and the true. But I will give you a clear indication which will make it impossible for you to go wrong or to doubt if some favour has come from God; His Majesty has put it into my mind only today, and I think it is quite decisive. In difficult matters, even if I believe I understand what I am saying and am speaking the truth, I use this phrase "I think," because, if I am mistaken, I am very ready to give credence to those who have great

44. Gracian substitutes "understanding" for "thoughts" and adds a marginal note: "This is (to be) understood of acts of the understanding and the will, for the thoughts of the imagination are clearly seen by the devil unless God blinds him in that respect." Luis de Leon included the marginal note in the text of his edition but Gracian did not reproduce it in either the text or the margin of the Cordoba copy, though he altered "thoughts" to "understanding."

45. Gracian inserts the word "nature" here, interlineally.

46. [P. Silverio refers here to Way of Perfection, Chap. XXXI, but I hardly think this can be meant. Perhaps the author's allusion is to the first chapter of the Fourth Mansions (p. 75, above) or possibly to something she once said viva voce.]

learning. For even if they have not themselves experienced these things, men of great learning have a certain instinct[47] to prompt them. As God uses them to give light to His Church, He reveals to them anything which is true so that it shall be accepted; and if they do not squander their talents, but are true servants of God, they will never be surprised at His greatness, for they know quite well that He is capable of working more and still more. In any case, where matters are in question for which there is no explanation, there must be others about which they can read, and they can deduce from their reading that it is possible for these firstnamed to have happened.

Of this I have the fullest experience; and I have also experience of timid, half-learned men whose shortcomings have cost me very dear. At any rate, my own opinion is that anyone who does not believe that God can do much more than this, and that He has been pleased, and is sometimes still pleased, to grant His creatures such favours, has closed the door fast against receiving them. Therefore, sisters, let this never be true of you, but trust God more and more, and do not consider whether those to whom He communicates His favours are bad or good. His Majesty knows all about this, as I have said; intervention on our part is quite unnecessary; rather must we serve His Majesty with humility and simplicity of heart, and praise Him for His works and wonders.

Turning now to the indication which I have described as[48] a decisive one: here is this soul which God has made, as it were, completely foolish in order the better to impress upon it true wisdom. For as long as such a soul is in this state, it can neither see nor hear nor understand: the period is always short and seems to the soul even shorter than it really is. God implants Himself in the interior of that soul in such a way that, when it returns to itself, it cannot[49] possibly doubt that God has been in it and it has been in God; so firmly does this truth remain within it that, although for years God may never grant it that favour again, it can neither forget it nor doubt that it has received it (and this quite apart from the effects which remain within it, and of which I will speak later). This certainty of the soul is very material.

But now you will say to me: How did the soul see it and

---

47. *[Lit.:* "a something": the Spanish is *un no se que,* an expression corresponding to the French *un je ne sais quoi.]*
48. Gracian alters "as" to "as being, I think."
49. Gracian inserts: "it thinks."

understand it if it can neither see nor understand? I am not saying that it saw it at the time,[50] but that it sees it clearly afterwards, and not because it is a vision, but because of a certainty which remains in the soul, which can be put there only by God. I know of a person who had not learned that God was in all things by presence and power and essence; God granted her a favour of this kind, which convinced her of this so firmly[51] that, although one of those half-learned men whom I have been talking about, and whom she asked in what way God was in us (until God granted him an understanding of it he knew as little of it as she), told her that He was in us only by grace, she had the truth so firmly implanted within her that she did not believe him, and asked others, who told her the truth, which was a great consolation to her.[52]

Do not make the mistake of thinking that this certainty has anything to do with bodily form—with the presence of Our Lord Jesus Christ, for example, unseen by us, in the Most Holy Sacrament. It has nothing to do with this—only with His Divinity. How, you will ask, can we become so convinced of what we have not seen? That I do not know; it is the work of God. But I know I am speaking the truth; and if anyone has not that certainty, I should say that what he has experienced is not union of the whole soul with God but only union of one of the faculties or some one of the many other kinds of favour which God grants the soul. In all these matters we must stop looking for reasons why they happened; if our understanding cannot grasp them, why should we try to perplex it? It suffices us to know that He Who brings this to pass is all-powerful,[53] and as it is God Who does it and we, however hard we work, are quite incapable of achieving it, let us not try to become capable of understanding it either.

With regard to what I have just said about our incapability, I recall that, as you have heard, the Bride in the *Songs* says: "The King brought me" (or "put me," I think the words are) "into the cellar of wine."[54] It does not say that she *went*. It also

50. Gracian amends the following phrase to read: "but that there has since remained with it, as it thinks, a certainty, etc."
51. Gracian alters this phrase to: "which made her understand this in such a way."
52. St. Teresa refers to this experience of hers in *Life*, Chap. XVIII (Image Books Edition, p. 180). Later, a favour which she received *(Relations*, LIV: Vol. I, p. 361.) enlightened her further on this point. According to Yepes (II, xx) she asked him for theological guidance about it just before she began the *Interior Castle*.
53. The rest of this paragraph was omitted by Luis de Leon.
54. Canticles i, 3; ii, 4. Gracian deletes the bracketed phrase but writes "put" above "brought."

says that she was wandering about in all directions seeking her Beloved.[55] This, as I understand it, is the cellar where the Lord is pleased to put us, when He wills and as He wills. But we cannot enter by any efforts of our own; His Majesty must put us right into the centre[56] of our soul, and must enter there Himself; and, in order that He may the better show us His wonders, it is His pleasure that our will, which has entirely surrendered itself to him, should have no part in this. Nor does He desire the door of the faculties and senses, which are all asleep, to be opened to Him; He will come into the centre of the soul without using a door, as He did when He came in to His disciples, and said *Pax vobis*,[57] and when He left the sepulchre without removing the stone. Later on you will see how it is His Majesty's will that the soul should have fruition of Him in its very centre, but you will be able to realize that in the last Mansion much better than here.

Oh, daughters, what a lot we shall see if we desire to see no more than our own baseness and wretchedness and to understand that we are not worthy to be the handmaidens of so great a Lord, since we cannot comprehend His marvels. May He be for ever praised. Amen.

Continues the same subject. Explains the Prayer of Union by a delicate comparison. Describes the effects which it produces in the soul. Should be studied with great care.

You will suppose that all there is to be seen in this Mansion has been described already, but there is much more to come yet, for, as I said, some receive more and some less. With regard to the nature of union, I do not think I can say anything further; but when the soul to which God grants these favours prepares itself for them, there are many things to be said concerning what the Lord works in it. Some of these I shall say now, and I shall describe that soul's state. In order the better to explain this, I will make use of a comparison which is suitable for the purpose; and which will also show us how, although this work is performed by the Lord, and we can do nothing to make His Majesty grant us this favour, we can do a great deal to prepare ourselves for it.

55. Canticles iii, 2.
56. Here and just below Gracian has crossed out the word "centre."
57. St. John xx, 19.

You will have heard of the wonderful way in which silk is made—a way which no one could invent but God—and how it comes from a kind of seed which looks like tiny peppercorns[58] (I have never seen this, but only heard of it, so if it is incorrect in any way the fault is not mine). When the warm weather comes, and the mulberry-trees begin to show leaf, this seed starts to take life; until it has this sustenance, on which it feeds, it is as dead. The silkworms feed on the mulberry-leaves until they are full-grown, when people put down twigs, upon which, with their tiny mouths, they start spinning silk, making themselves very tight little cocoons, in which they bury themselves. Then, finally, the worm, which was large and ugly, comes right out of the cocoon a beautiful white butterfly.

Now if no one had ever seen this, and we were only told about is as a story of past ages, who would believe it? And what arguments could we find to support the belief that a thing as devoid of reason as a worm or a bee could be diligent enough to work so industriously for our advantage, and that in such an enterprise the poor little worm would lose its life? This alone, sisters, even if I tell you no more, is sufficient for a brief meditation, for it will enable you to reflect upon the wonders and the wisdom of our God. What, then, would it be if we knew the properties of everything? It will be a great help to us if we occupy ourselves in thinking of these wonderful things and rejoice in being the brides of so wise and powerful a King.

But to return to what I was saying. The silkworm is like the soul which takes life when, through the heat which comes from the Holy Spirit, it begins to utilize the general help which God gives to us all, and to make use of the remedies which He left in His Church—such as frequent confessions, good books and sermons, for these are the remedies for a soul dead in negligences and sins and frequently plunged into temptation. The soul begins to live and nourishes itself on this food, and on good meditations, until it is full grown— and this is what concerns me now: the rest is of little importance.

When it is full-grown, then, as I wrote at the beginning, it starts to spin its silk and to build the house in which it is to die. This house may be understood here to mean Christ. I think I read or heard somewhere that our life is hid in Christ, or in God

---

58. "Mustard-seeds," writes Gracian, interlineally, deleting the bracketed sentence which follows and adding the words: "It is so, for I have seen it."

(for that is the same thing), or that our life is Christ.[59] (The exact form of this[60] is little to my purpose.)

Here, then, daughters, you see what we can do, with God's favour. May His Majesty Himself be our Mansion as He is in this Prayer of Union which, as it were, we ourselves spin. When I say He will be our Mansion, and we can construct it for ourselves and hide ourselves in it, I seem to be suggesting that we can subtract from God, or add to Him. But of course we cannot possibly do that! We can neither subtract from, nor add to, God, but we can subtract from, and add to, ourselves, just as these little silkworms do. And, before we have finished doing all that we can in that respect, God will take this tiny achievement of ours, which is nothing at all, unite it with His greatness and give it such worth that its reward will be the Lord Himself. And as it is He Whom it has cost the most, so His Majesty will unite our small trials with the great trials which He suffered, and make both of them into one.

Oh, then, my daughters! Let us hasten to perform this task and spin this cocoon. Let us renounce our self-love and self-will, and our attachment to earthly things. Let us practise penance, prayer, mortification, obedience, and all the other good works that you know of. Let us do what we have been taught; and we have been instructed about what our duty is. Let the silkworm die—let it die, as in fact it does when it has completed the work which it was created to do. Then we shall see God and shall ourselves be as completely hidden in His greatness as is this little worm in its cocoon. Note that, when I speak of seeing God, I am referring to the way in which, as I have said, He allows Himself to be apprehended in this kind of union.

And now let us see what becomes of this silkworm, for all that I have been saying about it is leading to this. When it is in this state of prayer, and quite dead to the world, it comes out a little white butterfly. Oh, greatness of God, that a soul should come out like this after being hidden in the greatness of God, and closely united with Him, for so short a time—never, I think, for as long as half an hour! I tell you truly, the very soul does not know itself. For think of the difference between an ugly worm and a white butterfly; it is just the same here. The soul cannot think how it can have merited such a blessing—whence

59. Colossians iii, 3. Gracian deletes "for that . . . my purpose" and supplies text and source in the margin.
60. [*Lit.*: "Whether this be so or not." But the meaning is clear from the context.]

such a blessing could have come to it, I meant to say, for it knows quite well that it has not merited it at all.[61] It finds itself so anxious to praise the Lord that it would gladly be consumed and die a thousand deaths for His sake. Then it finds itself longing to suffer great trials and unable to do otherwise. It has the most vehement desires for penance, for solitude, and for all to know God. And hence, when it sees God being offended, it becomes greatly distressed. In the following Mansion we shall treat of these things further and in detail, for, although the experiences of this Mansion and of the next are almost identical, their effects come to have much great power; for, as I have said, if after God comes to a soul here on earth it strives to progress still more, it will experience great things.

To see, then, the restlessness of this little butterfly—though it has never been quieter or more at rest in its life! Here is something to praise God for—namely, that it knows not where to settle and make its abode. By comparison with the abode it has had, everything it sees on earth leaves it dissatisfied, especially when God has again and again given it this wine which almost every time has brought it some new blessing. It sets no store by the things it did when it was a worm—that is, by its gradual weaving of the cocoon. It has wings now: how can it be content to crawl along slowly when it is able to fly? All that it can do for God seems to it slight by comparison with its desires. It even attaches little importance to what the saints endured, knowing by experience how the Lord helps and transforms a soul so that it seems no longer to be itself, or even its own likeness. For the weakness which it used to think it had when it came to doing penance is now turned into strength. It is no longer bound by ties of relationship, friendship or property. Previously all its acts of will and resolutions and desires were powerless to loosen these and seemed only to bind them the more firmly; now it is grieved at having even to fulfil its obligations in these respects lest these should cause it to sin against God. Everything wearies it, because it has proved that it can find no true rest in the creatures.

I seem to be enlarging on this subject and there is much more that I could say: anyone to whom God has granted this favour will realize that I have said very little. It is not surprising, then, that, as this little butterfly feels a stranger to things of the

---

61. The words "I meant . . . at all" are omitted from the *editio princeps*.

earth, it should be seeking a new resting place. But where will the poor little creature go? It cannot return to the place it came from, for, as has been said, however hard we try, it is not in our power to do that until God is pleased once again to grant us this favour. Ah, Lord! What trials begin afresh for this soul!

DARK NIGHT OF THE SOUL*
By St. John of the Cross

St. John of the Cross (1542-1591) and St. Teresa were close friends and the most noted Christian mystics of the post-Biblical era. These authors are the glory of Spanish Catholicism. St. John relates in this passage the positive meaning of the purifications that continue after the first series of mystic union experiences. The soul is now challenged to surrender itself to a deeper degree since it has been fortified with the spiritual graces of the first union experiences.

DARK NIGHT OF THE SOUL
How, although this night brings darkness to the spirit, it does so in order to illumine it and give it light.[62]

It now remains to be said that, although this happy night brings darkness to the spirit, it does so only to give it light in everything; and that, although it humbles it and makes it miserable, it does so only to exalt it and to raise it up; and, although it impoverishes it and empties it of all natural affection and attachment, it does so only that it may enable it to stretch forward, divinely, and thus to have fruition and experience of all things, both above and below, yet to preserve its unrestricted liberty of spirit in them all. For just as the elements, in order that they may have a part in all natural entities and compounds, must have no particular colour, odour or taste, so as to be able to combine with all tastes, odours and colours, just so must the spirit be simple, pure and detached from all kinds of natural affection, whether actual or habitual, to the end that it may be able freely to share in the breadth of spirit of the Divine Wisdom, wherein, through its purity, it has experience of all the sweetness of all things in a certain preeminently excellent way.[63] And without this purgation it will be wholly unable to feel or experience the satisfaction of all this abundance of spiritual sweetness. For one single affection remaining in the spirit, or one particular thing to which, actually or habitually, it clings, suffices to hinder it from

---

*Reprinted from *The Complete Works of St. John of the Cross,* translated and edited by E. Allison Peers, Westminster, Maryland, Newman, 1964, Vol. I, pp. 396-402. Used with permission of Search Press, London.

62. So e.p. The Codices have no title.

63. [*Lit.,* 'with a certain eminence of excellence.'] So C, H, M, Mtr., P, V, A, B, e.p.: 'certain kind of excellence.' Bz. omits a line or so here.

feeling or experiencing or communicating the delicacy and intimate sweetness of the spirit of love, which contains within itself all sweetness to a most eminent degree.[64]

For, even as the children of Israel, solely because they retained one single affection and remembrance—namely, with respect to the fleshpots and the meals which they had tasted in Egypt[65]—could not relish the delicate bread of angels, in the desert, which was the manna, which, as the Divine Scripture says, held sweetness for every taste and turned to the taste that each one desired;[66] even so the spirit cannot succeed in enjoying the delights of the spirit of liberty, according to the desire of the will, if it be still affectioned to any desire, whether actual or habitual, or to particular objects of understanding, or to any other apprehension.[67] The reason for this is that the affections, feelings and apprehensions of the perfect spirit, being Divine,[68] are of another kind and of a very different order from those that are natural. They are pre-eminent,[69] so that, in order both actually and habitually to possess the one, it is needful to expel and annihilate the other, as with two contrary things, which cannot exist together in one person.[70] Therefore it is most fitting and necessary, if the soul is to pass to these great things, that this dark night of contemplation should first of all annihilate and undo it in its meannesses, bringing it into darkness, aridity, affliction and emptiness; for the light which is to be given to it is a Divine light of the highest kind, which transcends all natural light, and which by nature can find no place in the understanding.

And thus it is fitting that, if the understanding is to be united with that light and become Divine in the state of perfection, it should first of all be purged and annihilated as to its natural light, and, by means of this dark contemplation, be brought actually into darkness. This darkness should continue for as long as is needful in order to expel and annihilate the habit which the soul has long since formed in its manner of understanding, and the Divine light and illumination will then take its place. And thus, inasmuch as that power of under-

---

64. [*Lit.*, '. . . sweetness, with great eminence.']
65. Exodus xvi, 3.
66. Wisdom xvi, 21.
67. Thus the Codices. E.p. has: 'any other limited apprehension.'
68. E.p.: 'being so high and very specially Divine.'
69. E.p. omits the last three words.
70. E.p. omits: 'as with . . . person.'

standing which it had aforetime is natural, it follows that the darkness which it here suffers is profound and horrible and most painful, for this darkness, being felt in the deepest substance of the spirit, seems to be substantial darkness.[71] Similarly, since the affection of love which is to be given to it in the Divine union of love is Divine, and therefore very spitirual, subtle and delicate, and very intimate, transcending every affection and feeling[72] of the will, and every desire thereof, it is fitting that, in order that the will may be able to attain to this Divine affection and most lofty delight, and to feel it and experience it[73] through the union of love, since it is not, in the way of nature, perceptible to the will,[74] it be first of all purged and annihilated in all its affections and feelings, and left in a condition of aridity and constraint, proportionate to the habit of natural affections which it had before, with respect both to Divine things and to human. Thus, being exhausted, withered and thoroughly tried[75] in the fire of this dark contemplation, and having driven away every kind[76] of evil spirit (as with the heart of the fish which Tobias set on the coals[77]), it may have a simple and pure disposition, and its palate may be purged and healthy, so that it may feel the rare and sublime touches of Divine love, wherein it will see itself divinely transformed, and all the contrarieties, whether actual or habitual, which it had aforetime, will be expelled, as we are saying.

Moreover, in order to attain the said union to which this dark night is disposing and leading it, the soul must be filled and endowed with a certain glorious magnificence in its communion with God, which includes within itself innumerable blessings springing from delights which exceed all the abundance that the soul can naturally possess. For by nature the soul is so weak and impure that it cannot receive all this. As Isaias says: 'Eye hath not seen, nor ear heard, neither hath it entered into the heart of man, that which God hath prepared,

71. E.p. reads: '. . . painful, for it touches, and is felt in, the depths of the spirit.'
72. E.p.: 'every natural imperfect affection and feeling.'
73. E.p. omits: 'feel it and.'
74. E.p. omits: 'since . . . will.'
75. So H. There are many variants. A: 'that it may be dry and withered and well proved.' B: 'that it may be dry, withered and well entangled *(sic).'* [Probably a copyist's error: *entrincada* for *extricada,* 'wrung.'] Bz.: 'that it may be withered and well bruised.' C, M, P: 'Thus, exhausted and withered and well wrung.' Mtr.: 'that it may be withered and well wrung.' V: 'that it may be clean and withered and well wrung.' E.p.: 'Thus, exhausted, withered and deprived (of every kind, etc.).'
76. [*Lit.,* 'from every kind.' But see Tobias viii, 2. The 'deprived' of e.p. gives the best reading of this phrase, but the general sense is clear from the Scriptural reference.]
77. Tobias viii, 2.

etc.'[78] It is meet, then, that the soul be first of all brought into emptiness and poverty of spirit and purged from all help, consolation and natural apprehension with respect to all things, both above and below. In this way, being empty, it is able indeed to be poor in spirit and freed from the old man, in order to live that new and blessed life which is attained by means of this night, and which is the state of union with God.

And because the soul is to attain to the possession of a sense, and of a Divine knowledge, which is very generous and full of sweetness, with respect to things Divine and human, which fall not within the common experience and natural knowledge of the soul (because it looks on them with eyes as different from those of the past as spirit is different from sense[79] and the Divine from the human), the spirit must be straitened[80] and inured to hardships as regards its common and natural experience, and be brought by means of this purgative contemplation into great anguish and affliction, and the memory must be borne far from all agreeable and peaceful knowledge, and have an intimate[81] sense and feeling that it is making a pilgrimage and being a stranger to all things, so that it seems to it that all things are strange and of a different kind from that which they were wont to be. For this night is gradually drawing the spirit away from its ordinary and common experience of things and bringing it nearer the Divine sense, which is a stranger and an alien to all human ways. It seems now to the soul that it is going forth from its very self, with much affliction.[82] At other times it wonders if it is under a charm or a spell, and it goes about marvelling at the things that it sees and hears, which seem to it very strange and rare, though they are the same that it was accustomed to experience aforetime. The reason of this is that the soul is now becoming alien and remote from common sense and knowledge of things, in order that, being annihilated in this respect, it may be informed with the Divine—which belongs rather to the next life than to this.

The soul suffers all these afflictive purgations[83] of the spirit to the end that it may be begotten anew in spiritual life by

78. Isaias lxiv, 4 [1 Corinthians ii, 9]. E.p. adds: 'for those that love Him.'
79. E.p.: 'as the light and grace of the Holy Spirit differ from sense.'
80. [*Lit.*, 'be made thin.']
81. E.p.: 'a very intimate.'
82. A, e.p.: '. . . human ways; so much so that it seems to the soul that it is going out from its very self.' So M, omitting the words 'much so.' B, Bz., C, H, V read as in the text.
83. A, B, M, Mtr., P: 'all these afflictions and purgations.' Bz., C: 'affective purgations.'

means of this Divine inflowing, and in these pangs may bring forth the spirit of salvation, that the saying of Isaias may be fulfilled: 'In Thy sight, O Lord, we have conceived, and we have been as in the pangs of labour, and we have brought forth the spirit of salvation.'[84] Moreover, since by means of this contemplative night the soul is prepared for the attainment of inward peace and tranquillity, which is of such a kind and so delectable that, as the Scripture[85] says, it passes all understanding,[86] it behoves the soul to abandon all its former peace. This was in reality no peace at all, since it was involved in imperfections; but to the soul aforementioned it appeared to be so, because it was following its own inclinations, which were for peace. It seemed, indeed, to be a twofold peace—that is, the soul believed that it had already acquired the peace of sense and that of spirit, for it found itself to be full of the spiritual abundance of this peace of sense and of spirit—as I say, it is still imperfect. First of all, then, it must be purged of that former peace and disquieted concerning it and withdrawn from it.[87] Even so was Jeremias when, in the passage which we quoted from him, he felt and lamented[88] thus, in order to express the calamities of this night that is past, saying: 'My soul is withdrawn and removed from peace.'[89]

This is a painful disturbance, involving many misgivings, imaginings and strivings which the soul has within itself, wherein, with the apprehension and realization of the miseries in which it sees itself, it fancies that it is lost and that its blessings have gone for ever. Wherefore the spirit experiences[90] pain and sighing so deep that they cause it vehement spiritual groans and cries, to which at times it gives vocal expression; when it has the necessary strength and power it dissolves into tears, although this relief comes but seldom. David[91] describes this very aptly, in a Psalm, as one who has had experience of it, where he says: 'I was exceedingly afflicted and humbled; I

84. Isaias xxvi, 17-18.
85. [P. Silverio reads, with] A, B, M: 'the gloss.' [This was probably what the Saint actually wrote.] Bz., C, H, Mtr., P [not understanding it] have: 'the Church' [la Iglesia for la Glosa]. V, e.p. [give the correct sense by reading]: 'the Scripture.'
86. [Philippians iv, 7.]
87. [We have here split up a parenthesis of about seventy words.] E.p. abbreviates: '[It seemed to be] a twofold peace, that is, of sense and spirit. First of all it must be purged that it may be disquieted concerning that imperfect peace, and withdrawn from it.'
88. [Lit., 'and wept.']
89. Lamentations iii, 17.
90. So C, H, Mtr., P, V. The other Codices and e.p. read: 'Wherefore there has entered into the spirit.'
91. E.p.: 'The royal prophet David.'

roared with the groaning of my heart.'[92] This roaring implies great pain; for at times, with the sudden and acute remembrance of these miseries wherein the soul sees itself, pain and affliction rise up and surround it, and I know not how the affections of the soul could be described[93] save in the similitude of holy Job, when he was in the same trials, and uttered these words: 'Even as the overflowing of the waters, even so is my roaring.'[94] For just as at times the waters make such inundations that they overwhelm and fill everything, so at times this roaring and this affliction of the soul grow to such an extent that they overwhelm it and penetrate it completely, filling it with spiritual pain and anguish in all its deep affections and energies, to an extent surpassing all possibility of exaggeration.

Such is the work wrought in the soul by this night that hides the hopes of the light of day. With regard to this the prophet Job says likewise: 'In the night my mouth is pierced with sorrows and they that feed upon me sleep not.'[95] Now here by the mouth is understood the will, which is transpierced with these pains that tear the soul to pieces, neither ceasing nor sleeping, for the doubts and misgivings which transpierce the soul in this way never cease.[96]

Deep in this warfare and this striving, for the peace which the soul hopes for will be very deep; and the spiritual pain is intimate and delicate,[97] for the love which it will possess will likewise be very intimate and refined. The more intimate and the more perfect the finished work is to be and to remain, the more intimate, perfect and pure must be the labour; the firmer the edifice, the harder the labour.[98] Wherefore, as Job says, the soul is fading within itself, and its vitals are being consumed without any hope.[99] Similarly, because in the state of perfection toward which it journeys by means of this purgative night the soul will attain to the possession and fruition of innumerable blessings, of gifts and virtues, both according to

---

92. Psalm xxxvii, 9 [A.V., xxxviii, 8].
93. [*Lit.*, '. . . sees itself, it arises and is surrounded with pain and affliction, the affections of the soul, that I know not how it could be described.' A confused, ungrammatical sentence, of which, however, the general meaning is not doubtful.] E.p. has: '. . . sees itself, the affections of the soul feels [*sic*] such pain and affliction.'
94. Job iii, 24.
95. Job xxx, 17.
96. H: 'never sleep.'
97. E.p. adds: 'and refined.'
98. Some MSS. omit the words 'the labour,' but the meaning is evidently the same.
99. Job xxx, 16.

the substance of the soul and likewise[100] according to its faculties, it must needs see and feel itself withdrawn from them all and deprived of them all and be empty and poor without them;[101] and it must needs believe itself to be so far from them that it cannot persuade itself that it will ever reach them, but rather it must be convinced that all its good things are over. The words of Jeremias have a similar meaning in that passage already quoted, where he says: 'I have forgotten good things.'[102]

But let us now see the reason why this light of contemplation, which is so sweet and blessed to the soul that there is naught more desirable (for, as has been said above, it is the same wherewith the soul must be united and wherein it must find all the good things in the state of perfection that it desires), produces, when it assails the soul, these beginnings which are so painful and these effects which are so disagreeable, as we have here said.

This question is easy for us to answer, by explaining, as we have already done in part, that the cause of this is that, in contemplation and the Divine inflowing, there is naught that of itself can cause affliction, but that they rather cause great sweetness and delight, as we shall say hereafter.[103] The cause is rather the weakness and imperfection from which the soul then suffers, and the dispositions which it has in itself and which make it unfit for the reception of them. Wherefore, when[104] the said Divine light assails the soul, it must needs cause it to suffer after the manner aforesaid.

---

100. E.p. omits 'likewise.'
101. E.p. omits: 'and be empty . . . them.'
102. Lamentations iii, 17.
103. So Bz., C, H, Mtr. A, B, M: 'as was [*sic*] afterwards given it.' E.p.: 'as will afterwards be given it.' V: 'as was said before.'
104. E.p. 'unfit [*lit.*, 'contrary': this also applies to our text] for the reception of that sweetness. And thus, when,' etc.

WAITING FOR GOD*
By Simone Weil

Simone Weil is one of the most important spiritual writers of our century. She embraced Christianity but could not belong to a church, believing churches build walls instead of bridges. The following is an explanation of Simone's meaning of affliction and where it leads one.

WAITING FOR GOD

Affliction makes God appear to be absent for a time, more absent than a dead man, more absent than light in the utter darkness of a cell. A kind of horror submerges the whole soul. During this absence there is nothing to love. What is terrible is that if, in this darkness where there is nothing to love, the soul ceases to love, God's absence becomes final. The soul has to go on loving in the emptiness, or at least to go on wanting to love, though it may only be with an infinitesimal part of itself. Then, one day, God will come to show himself to this soul and to reveal the beauty of the world to it, as in the case of Job. But if the soul stops loving it falls, even in this life, into something almost equivalent to hell.

One can only accept the existence of affliction by considering it at a distance.

God created through love and for love. God did not create anything except love itself, and the means to love. He created love in all its forms. He created beings capable of love from all possible distances. Because no other could do it, he himself went to the greatest possible distance, the infinite distance. This infinite distance between God and God, this supreme tearing apart, this agony beyond all others, this marvel of love, is the crucifixion. Nothing can be further from God than that which has been made accursed.

This tearing apart, over which supreme love places the bond of supreme union, echoes perpetually across the universe in the midst of the silence, like two notes, separate yet melting into one, like pure and heart-rending harmony. This is the Word of God. The whole creation is nothing but its vibration. When

*Reprinted by permission of G.P. Putnam's Sons from *Waiting for God* by Simone Weil, translated by Emma Craufurd. Copyright 1951 by G.P. Putnam's Sons, pp. 120 and 123-136.

human music in its greatest purity pierces our soul, this is what we hear through it. When we have learned to hear the silence, this is what we grasp more distinctly through it.

Those who persevere in love hear this note from the very lowest depths into which affliction has thrust them. From that moment they can no longer have any doubt.

Men struck down by affliction are at the foot of the Cross, almost at the greatest possible distance from God. It must not be thought that sin is a greater distance. Sin is not a distance, it is a turning of our gaze in the wrong direction.

It is true that there is a mysterious connection between this distance and an original disobedience. From the beginning, we are told, humanity turned its gaze away from God and walked in the wrong direction for as far as it could go. That was because it could walk then. As for us, we are nailed down to the spot, only free to choose which way we look, ruled by necessity. A blind mechanism, heedless of degrees of spiritual perfection, continually tosses men about and throws some of them at the very foot of the Cross. It rests with them to keep or not to keep their eyes turned toward God through all the jolting. It does not mean that God's Providence is lacking. It is in his Providence that God has willed that necessity should be like a blind mechanism.

If the mechanism were not blind there would not be any affliction. Affliction is anonymous before all things; it deprives its victims of their personality and makes them into things. It is indifferent; and it is the coldness of this indifference—a metallic coldness—that freezes all those it touches right to the depths of their souls. They will never find warmth again. They will never believe any more that they are anyone.

Affliction would not have this power without the element of chance contained by it. Those who are persecuted for their faith and are aware of the fact are not afflicted, although they have to suffer. They only fall into a state of affliction if suffering or fear fills the soul to the point of making it forget the cause of the persecution. The martyrs who entered the arena, singing as they went to face the wild beasts, were not afflicted. Christ was afflicted. He did not die like a martyr. He died like a common criminal, confused with thieves, only a little more ridiculous. For affliction is ridiculous.

Only blind necessity can throw men to the extreme point of distance, right next to the Cross. Human crime, which is the cause of most affliction, is part of blind necessity, because criminals do not know what they are doing.

There are two forms of friendship: meeting and separation. They are indissoluble. Both of them contain some good, and this good of friendship is unique, for when two beings who are not friends are near each other there is no meeting, and when friends are far apart there is no separation. As both forms contain the same good thing, they are both equally good.

God produces himself and knows himself perfectly, just as we in our miserable fashion make and know objects outside ourselves. But, before all things, God is love. Before all things God loves himself. This love, this friendship of God, is the Trinity. Between the terms united by this relation of divine love there is more than nearness; there is infinite nearness or identity. But, resulting from the Creation, the Incarnation, and the Passion, there is also infinite distance. The totality of space and the totality of time, interposing their immensity, put an infinite distance between God and God.

Lovers or friends desire two things. The one is to love each other so much that they enter into each other and only make one being. The other is to love each other so much that, with half the globe between them, their union will not be diminished in the slightest degree. All that man vainly desires here below is perfectly realized in God. We have all those impossible desires within us as a mark of our destination, and they are good for us when we no longer hope to accomplish them.

The love between God and God, which in itself *is* God, is this bond of double virtue: the bond that unites two beings so closely that they are no longer distinguishable and really form a single unity and the bond that stretches across distance and triumphs over infinite separation. The unity of God, wherein all plurality disappears, and the abandonment, wherein Christ believes he is left while never ceasing to love his Father perfectly, these are two forms expressing the divine virtue of the same Love, the Love that is God himself.

God is so essentially love that the unity, which in a sense is his actual definition, is the pure effect of love. Moreover, corresponding to the infinite virtue of unification belonging to this love, there is the infinite separation over which it triumphs, which is the whole creation spread throughout the totality of space and time, made of mechanically harsh matter and interposed between Christ and his Father.

As for us men, our misery gives us the infinitely precious privilege of sharing in this distance placed between the Son and his Father. This distance is only separation, however, for those who love. For those who love, separation, although painful, is a good, because it is love. Even the distress of the abandoned Christ is a good. There cannot be a greater good for us on earth than to share in it. God can never be perfectly present to us here below on account of our flesh. But he can be almost perfectly absent from us in extreme affliction. This is the only possibility of perfection for us on earth. That is why the Cross is our only hope. "No forest bears such a tree, with such blossoms, such foliage, and such fruit."

This universe where we are living, and of which we form a tiny particle, is the distance put by Love between God and God. We are a point in this distance. Space, time, and the mechanism that governs matter are the distance. Everything that we call evil is only this mechanism. God has provided that when his grace penetrates to the very center of a man and from there illuminates all his being, he is able to walk on the water without violating any of the laws of nature. When, however, a man turns away from God, he simply gives himself up to the law of gravity. Then he thinks that he can decide and choose, but he is only a thing, a stone that falls. If we examine human society and souls closely and with real attention, we see that wherever the virtue of supernatural light is absent, everything is obedient to mechanical laws as blind and as exact as the laws of gravitation. To know this is profitable and necessary. Those whom we call criminals are only tiles blown off a roof by the wind and falling at random. Their only fault is the initial choice by which they became such tiles.

The mechanism of necessity can be transposed to any level while still remaining true to itself. It is the same in the world of pure matter, in the animal world, among nations, and in souls. Seen from our present standpoint, and in human perspective, it is quite blind. If, however, we transport our hearts beyond ourselves, beyond the universe, beyond space and time to where our Father dwells, and if from there we behold this mechanism, it appears quite different. What seemed to be necessity becomes obedience. Matter is entirely passive and in consequence entirely obedient to God's will. It is a perfect model for us. There cannot be any being other than God and that which obeys God. On account of its perfect obedience, matter deserves to be loved by those who love its Master, in the same way as a needle, handled by the beloved wife he has lost, is cherished by a lover. The beauty of the world gives us an intimation of its claim to a place in our heart. In the beauty of the world brute necessity becomes an object of love. What is more beautiful than the action of gravity on the fugitive folds of the sea waves, or on the almost eternal folds of the mountains?

The sea is not less beautiful in our eyes because we know that sometimes ships are wrecked by it. On the contrary, this adds to its beauty. If it altered the movement of its waves to spare a boat, it would be a creature gifted with discernment and choice and not this fluid, perfectly obedient to every external pressure. It is this perfect obedience that constitutes the sea's beauty.

All the horrors produced in this world are like the folds imposed upon the waves by gravity. That is why they contain an element of beauty. Sometimes a poem, such as the *Iliad,* brings this beauty to light.

Men can never escape from obedience to God. A creature cannot but obey. The only choice given to men, as intelligent and free creatures, is to desire obedience or not to desire it. If a man does not desire it, he obeys nevertheless, perpetually, inasmuch as he is a thing subject to mechanical necessity. If he desires it, he is still subject to mechanical necessity, but a new necessity is added to it, a necessity constituted by laws belonging to supernatural things. Certain actions become impossible for him; others are done by his agency, sometimes almost in spite of himself.

When we have the feeling that on some occasion we have disobeyed God, it simply means that for a time we have ceased to desire obedience. Of course it must be understood that, where everything else is equal, a man does not perform the same actions if he gives his consent to obedience as if he does not; just as a plant, where everything else is equal, does not grow in the same way in the light as in the dark.

The plant does not have any control or choice in the matter of its own growth. As for us, we are like plants that have the one choice of being in or out of the light.

Joy and suffering are two equally precious gifts, both of which must be savored to the full, each one in its purity, without trying to mix them. Through joy, the beauty of the world penetrates our soul. Through suffering it penetrates our body. We could no more become friends of God through joy alone than one becomes a ship's captain by studying books on navigation. The body plays a part in all apprenticeships. On the plane of physical sensibility, suffering alone gives us contact with that necessity which constitutes the order of the world, for pleasure does not involve an impression of necessity. It is a higher kind of sensibility, capable of recognizing a necessity in joy, and that only indirectly through a sense of beauty. In order that our being should one day become wholly sensitive in every part to this obedience that is the substance of matter, in order that a new sense should be formed in us to enable us to hear the universe as the vibration of the word of God, the transforming power of suffering and of joy are equally indispensable. When either of them comes to us we have to open the very center of our soul to it, just as a woman opens her door to messengers from her loved one. What does it matter to a lover if the messenger be polite or rough, so long as he delivers the message?

But affliction is not suffering. Affliction is something quite distinct from a method of God's teaching.

The infinity of space and time separates us from God. How are we to seek for him? How are we to go toward him? Even if we were to walk for hundreds of years, we should do no more than go round and round the world. Even in an airplane we could not do anything else. We are incapable of progressing vertically. We cannot take a step toward the heavens. God crosses the universe and comes to us.

Over the infinity of space and time, the infinitely more infinite love of God comes to possess us. He comes at his own time. We have the power to consent to receive him or to refuse. If we remain deaf, he comes back again and again like a beggar, but also, like a beggar, one day he stops coming. If we consent, God puts a little seed in us and he goes away again. From that moment God has no more to do; neither have we, except to wait. We only have not to regret the consent we gave him, the nuptial yes. It is not as easy as it seems, for the growth of the seed within us is painful. Moreover, from the very fact that we accept this growth, we cannot avoid destroying whatever gets in its way, pulling up the weeds, cutting the good grass, and unfortunately the good grass is part of our very flesh, so that this gardening amounts to a violent operation. On the whole, however, the seed grows of itself. A day comes when the soul belongs to God, when it not only consents to love but when truly and effectively it loves. Then in its turn it must cross the universe to go to God. The soul does not love like a creature with created love. The love within it is divine, uncreated; for it is the love of God for God that is passing through it. God alone is capable of loving God. We can only consent to give up our own feelings so as to allow free passage in our soul for this love. That is the meaning of denying oneself. We are created for this consent, and for this alone.

Divine Love crossed the infinity of space and time to come from God to us. But how can it repeat the journey in the opposite direction, starting from a finite creature? When the seed of divine love placed in us has grown and become a tree, how can we, we who bear it, take it back to its origin? How can we repeat the journey made by God when he came to us, in the opposite direction? How can we cross infinite distance?

It seems impossible, but there is a way—a way with which we are familiar. We know quite well in what likeness this tree is made, this tree that has grown within us, this most beautiful tree where the birds of the air come and perch. We know what is the most beautiful of all trees. "No forest bears its equal." Something still a little more frightful than a gibbet—that is the most beautiful of all trees. It was the seed of this tree that God placed within us, without our knowing what seed it was. If we had known, we should not have said yes at the first moment. It is this tree that has grown within us and has become ineradicable. Only a betrayal could uproot it.

When we hit a nail with a hammer, the whole of the shock received by the large head of the nail passes into the point without any of it being lost, although it is only a point. If the hammer and the head of the nail were infinitely big it would be just the same. The point of the nail would transmit this infinite shock at the point to which it was applied.

Extreme affliction, which means physical pain, distress of soul, and social degradation, all at the same time, is a nail whose point is applied at the very center of the soul, whose head is all necessity spreading throughout space and time.

Affliction is a marvel of divine technique. It is a simple and ingenious device which introduces into the soul of a finite creature the immensity of force, blind, brutal, and cold. The infinite distance separating God from the creature is entirely concentrated into one point to pierce the soul in its center.

The man to whom such a thing happens has no part in the operation. He struggles like a butterfly pinned alive into an album. But through all the horror he can continue to want to love. There is nothing impossible in that, no obstacle, one might almost say no difficulty. For the greatest suffering, so long as it does not cause the soul to faint, does not touch the acquiescent part of the soul, consenting to a right direction.

It is only necessary to know that love is a direction and not a state of the soul. If one is unaware of this, one falls into despair at the first onslaught of affliction.

He whose soul remains ever turned toward God though the nail pierces it finds himself nailed to the very center of the universe. It is the true center; it is not in the middle; it is beyond space and time; it is God. In a dimension that does not belong to space, that is not time, that is indeed quite a different dimension, this nail has pierced cleanly through all creation, through the thickness of the screen separating the soul from God.

In this marvelous dimension, the soul, without leaving the place and the instant where the body to which it is united is situated, can cross totality of space and time and come into the very presence of God.

It is at the intersection of creation and its Creator. This point of intersection is the point of intersection of the arms of the Cross.

Saint Paul was perhaps thinking about things of this kind when he said: "That ye, being rooted and grounded in love, may be able to comprehend with all saints and what is the breadth, and length, and depth, and height; and to know the love of Christ, which passeth knowledge."[105]

105. Epistle to the Ephesians 3:17-19.

Ecstatic Love

Part III

ECSTATIC LOVE

The progression in the sanctified life leads to deep experiences in union with God. It is an exceedingly great gift, says Brother Lawrence, to be united with God in this time of exile. Yet those who receive the gift are usually those who have struggled through aridities, darkness and sin. But they have not let anything defeat them, not even sin. Mystical union is not a miraculous state. It is merely the perfection of ordinary supernatural prayer; ordinary in the sense that God ordinarily gives it to those who remove obstacles and take the requisite means.[106]

Perhaps the most important single element in the Christian becoming process is the desire for God. One mystic has said that all good is done more or less by God's grace, the grace being in proportion to the greatness of the good. Since the greatest good, contemplation, is completely a gift of God, man being receptive in the mystical experience must try to do his share, so to speak, in the realm of the lower good. If a strong desire is the most important active part man can assume in the process of contemplation, the possession of that desire, or even the desire of that desire, will indicate to God that man is doing his utmost to ready himself for God's gift.[107]

Apart from the personal fulfillment of the mystical state, the community of Christian believers benefit from one who has received such a gift, for the mystic is their charismatic teacher. Evelyn Underhill writes that the mystics are the greatest of all teachers of prayer, and that we must learn from them if we wish to grow into mature men and women of God. They are the prophets of the church, enriching it with their writings on their experiences of God. In reading them, as in reading great poetry, we are taken out of ourselves, and become aware of deep regions of truth and beauty still beyond our reach. The Reality they are trying to show us is the same Reality which is the object of our faith; but we see through a glass darkly, and they, in their moments, face to face.[108]

What exactly is Christian mysticism? It is simply a direct

---

106. Lancelot Sheppard, *Spiritual Writers in Modern Times* (New York: Hawthorn Books, 1967), p. 18.

107. J.E. Milosh, *The Scale of Perfection and the English Mystical Tradition,* Madison, Wis.: University of Wisconsin Press, 1966), p. 53.

108. Evelyn Underhill, *The Mystics of the Church* (New York: Schocken Books, 1964), p. 12.

experience of love and joy in which God unites himself in varying degrees with his disciple, leaving him intensely stimulated and yet deeply humbled. It is a foretaste of the joys that are to be fully realized in the next life. Thomas Merton calls the mystical awakening our true birth. Martin Buber believes it is not only the decisive moment for man, but that without it man is unfit for the work of the spirit.

The mystical awakening is a revolutionary experience: it transforms one into a contemplative. One of the many results of God's gift of himself to his creatures is the soul's thirst and preoccupation for his God. The soul in an instant has tasted life's meaning and now longs after assimilation in the fulfillment of his discovery. Consequently, life has deeper dimensions and meaning than heretofore imagined. The soul, although in a quandary concerning the mystery of the experience, is nevertheless certain of and grateful for its happening.

The noted psychologist William James proposed that an experience be called mystical only when it possesses these characteristics: (1) ineffability, that is, it cannot be totally explained to one who has not had the experience; (2) noetic quality, meaning that a person has absolute certainty concerning his experience; (3) passivity, denoting that the person is acted upon rather than acting himself; and (4) transiency, indicating that the mystical state rarely lasts for any notable length of time.[109]

Many modern theologians believe that mysticism is not an esoteric phenomenon but that it is the ordinary intensification or the becoming of the Christian life. William Johnston writes: "These theologians insist that it is just a deepening of that faith and love that every true Christian possesses. They regard the mystic as a believer who loves God so intensely that his charity takes on a highly experimental character, coming to possess his whole being; and if their theory is correct, then every convinced believer is a mystic in embryo."[110]

After the testing and trials of discipleship and the "Dark Night" in which the soul has surrendered its will to the divine, the fullness of the mystical life is given. This fullness is called ecstasy. Ecstasy is a time when God ravished the soul with his

109. William James, *Varieties of the Religious Experience* (New York: Longman Green and Co. 1903), p. 114.
110. William Johnston, *The Stillpoint* (New York: Fordham University Press 1970), p. 125.

gifts of joy, love and peace. The soul is in bliss in its absorption in the divine. The body seems abandoned and the senses are suspended while the soul transcends the sphere of its natural operations and participates in supernatural life. St. Paul indicates this absorption when he says his ecstasy was such that he did not know whether he was in his body or out of the body. St. Teresa says that God unites himself with the soul in such a way that none can understand it save God and the soul, and even the soul afterwards cannot explain it. The graces of ecstasy are not habitual but transitory. They usher in the maturity of the mystic state.

Every man is called to journey back to God in faith. The mystical life is nothing other than the approaching end of this journey. God is now the object of one's contemplation and preoccupation. All creation is seen as unity and progression in Him. Mystical knowledge reveals the illusion of man's inability to be satisfied with anything but the divine. Mystical ecstasy is a partial knowledge through experience of this truth. The spiritual journey began with the leap of faith, progressed through prayer and charity and culminated in experiences of the knowledge of God's love for man. These experiences if only partial and transitory in this life anticipate eternity.

The first selection of mystical ecstasy is taken from Scripture. Again St. Paul dominates the language and descriptions of ecstasy. Future Christian mystics will look back to him in describing their own experiences. In Paul one sees the moral struggles and purifications, the slow self conquest and the deep insights characteristic of the developing life of prayer. Augustine, early Christianity's great philosopher-mystic next describes his spiritual experiences. The significance of Augustine is twofold. First, he was a great natural mystic, with remarkable power of self-analysis and expression; he has left us one of the most marvellous records in history of the transformation of a soul by God. Next, he brought Greek thought and religious feeling into the mainstream of Christian mysticism, thus giving it a color that it has never lost.[111]

Bernard of Clairvaux, the great medieval mystic, relates his spiritual experience as a type of communion between God and man. Bernard's influence was so great that it colored the whole spiritual life of the medieval church. His contemporary,

111. Underhill, *op. cit.* p. 60.

Richard of St. Victor, follows and gives one of the most beautiful examples of the degrees of spiritual love. More read than any other mystic, Teresa of Avila relates the next classic account of mystical ecstasy. Teresa's ecstatic experience never stopped her from practical undertakings. The very object of her soul's union with God was as she said in a memorable passage, work, work, work.

The Renaissance produced a whole cultural climate for mystical reality. This was particularly true in the Rhineland and England in the fourteenth century. Out of the Rhineland came John Ruysbroeck who some assert is the greatest mystic of the Christian church. Ruysbroeck is both speculative and practical. He must be read slowly for every phrase is full of meaning. The following selection is one brief example of what rapture is. In England, Julian of Norwich produced one of the most unique testimonies of mysticism. She believed she received her spiritual revelations in one episode rather than over a period of time. The following meditations are from her experience. The last selection is from St. John of the Cross, a mystical poet. St. John already introduced as the friend of St. Teresa and a brilliant mystical writer, relates in this selection a poem of mystical ecstasy.

SCRIPTURE
from the GOOD NEWS FOR MODERN MAN
American Bible Society, 1971

The Scriptural accounts of ecstasy are again found in St. Paul and St. John. Paul speaks about having been put to death with Christ and now lives within Him. Paul longs to be with Christ in heaven yet remains in the body for the church's sake. Paul's ecstasy was such that he was taken to paradise and saw and heard things that he cannot speak about to other men. St. John's gospel relates that those who live in love live in God and God lives within them.

SCRIPTURE

I have been put to death with Christ on his cross, so that it is no longer I who live, but it is Christ who lives in me. This life that I live now, I live by faith in the Son of God, who loved me and gave his life for me. I do not reject the grace of God. If a man is put right with God through the Law, it means that Christ died for nothing! *Galatians 2, 3*

For me, life means Christ; death is a prize to be won. But what if living on in this mortal body is the only way to harvest what I have sown? Thus I cannot tell what to choose; I am hemmed in on both sides. I long to have done with it, and be with Christ, a better thing, much more than a better thing; and yet, for your sakes, that I should wait in the body is more urgent still. *Philippians 1, 21-24*

I have to boast, even though it doesn't do any good. But I will now talk about visions and revelations given me by the Lord. I know a certain Christian man who fourteen years ago was snatched up to the highest heaven (I do not know whether this actually happened, or whether he had a vision—only God knows). I repeat, I know that this man was snatched to Paradise (again, I do not know whether this actually happened or whether it was a vision—only God knows), and there he heard things which cannot be put into words, things that human lips may not speak. *2 Corinthians 12*

Dear friends! Let us love one another, because love comes from God. Whoever loves is a child of God and knows God. Whoever does not love does not know God, because God is love. This is how God showed his love for us: he sent his only Son into the world that we might have life through him. This is what love is: it is not that we have loved God, but that he loved us and sent his Son to be the means by which our sins are forgiven.

Dear friends, if this is how God loved us, then we should love one another. No one has ever seen God; if we love one another, God lives in us and his love is made perfect in us.

This is how we are sure that we live in God and he lives in us: he has given us his Spirit. And we have seen and tell others that the Father sent his Son to be the Savior of the world. Whoever declares that Jesus is the Son of God, God lives in him, and he lives in God. And we ourselves know and believe in the love which God has for us.

God is love, and whoever lives in love lives in God and God lives in him. The purpose of love being made perfect in us is that we may have courage on Judgment Day: and we will have it because our life in this world is the same as Christ's. There is no fear in love: perfect love drives out all fear. So then, love has not been made perfect in the one who fears, because fear has to do with punishment.

I John 4

THE CONFESSIONS OF ST. AUGUSTINE*
Trans. by F. J. Sheed

For a thousand years after his death, Augustine's (354-430) influence was almost Biblical. He is the most noted of the Western church fathers and has had an important influence on Reformation theologies. He was a very human saint living during the collapse of the Roman Empire. The following auto-biographical passages trace Augustine's continual mystical enlightenment.

THE CONFESSIONS OF ST. AUGUSTINE

Being admonished by all this to return to myself, I entered into my own depths, with You as guide; and I was able to do it because You were my helper. I entered, and with the eye of my soul, such as it was, I saw Your unchangeable Light shining over that same eye of my soul, over my mind. It was not the light of everyday that the eye of flesh can see, nor some greater light of the same order, such as might be if the brightness of our daily light should be seen shining with a more intense brightness and filling all things with its greatness. Your Light was not that, but other, altogether other, that all such lights. Nor was it above my mind as oil above the water it floats on, nor as the sky is above the earth; it was above because it made me, and I was below because made by it. He who knows the truth knows that Light, and he that knows the Light knows eternity. Charity knows it. O eternal truth and true love and beloved eternity! Thou art my God, I sigh to Thee by day and by night. When first I knew Thee, Thou didst lift me up so that I might see that there was something to see, but that I was not yet the man to see it. And Thou didst beat back the weakness of my gaze, blazing upon me too strongly, and I was shaken with love and with dread. And I knew that I was far from Thee in the region of unlikeness, as if I heard Thy voice from on high: "I am the food of grown men: grow and you shall eat Me. And you shall not change Me into yourself as bodily food, but into Me you shall be changed." And I learned that *Thou hast corrected man for iniquity and Thou didst make my soul shrivel up like a moth.* And I said "Is truth then nothing at all, since it is not

*Reprinted with permission, © 1943, renewed 1970, by Sheed and Ward, Inc., New York, pp. 145, 149-151, 183, 190, 233, 234, 235, 236.

extended either through finite spaces or infinite?" And Thou didst cry to me from afar: "I am who am." And I heard Thee, as one hears in the heart; and there was from that moment no ground of doubt in me: I would more easily have doubted my own life than have doubted that truth is: which is *clearly seen, being understood by the things that are made.*

And I marvelled to find that at least I loved You and not some phantom instead of You; yet I did not stably enjoy my God, but was ravished to You by Your beauty, yet soon was torn away from You again by my own weight, and fell again with torment to lower things. Carnal habit was that weight. Yet the memory of You remained with me and I knew without doubt that it was You to whom I should cleave, though I was not yet such as could cleave to You: *for the corruptible body is a load upon the soul, and the earthly habitation presses down the mind that muses upon many things.* I was altogether certain that Your *invisible things are clearly seen from the creation of the world, being understood by the things that are made:* so too are Your everlasting power and Your Godhead. I was now studying the ground of my admiration for the beauty of bodies, whether celestial or of earth, and on what authority I might rightly judge of things mutable and say: "This ought to be so, that not so." Enquiring then what was the source of my judgment, when I did so judge I had discovered the immutable and true eternity of truth above my changing mind. Thus by stages I passed from bodies to the soul which uses the body for its perceiving, and from this to the soul's inner power, to which the body's senses present external things, as indeed the beasts are able; and from there I passed on to the reasoning power, to which is referred for judgment what is received from the body's senses. This too realised that it was mutable in me, and rose to its own understanding. It withdrew my thought from its habitual way, abstracting from the confused crowds of fantasms that it might find what light suffused it, when with utter certainty it cried aloud that the immutable was to be preferred to the mutable, and how it had come to know the immutable itself: for if it had not come to some knowledge of the immutable, it could not have known it as certainly preferable to the mutable. Thus in the thrust of a trembling glance my mind arrived at That Which Is. Then indeed I saw clearly Your *invisible things which are understood by the things that are made;* but I lacked the strength to hold my gaze fixed, and my weakness was beaten back again so that I returned to my old habits, bearing nothing with me but a memory of delight and a desire as for something of which I had caught the fragrance but which I had not yet the strength to eat.

So I set about finding a way to gain the strength that was necessary for enjoying You. And I could not find it until I embraced the *Mediator between God and man, the man Christ Jesus, who is over all things, God blessed forever,* who was calling unto me and saying: *I am the Way, the Truth, and the Life;* and who brought into union with our nature that Food which I lacked the strength to take: for *the Word was made flesh* that Your Wisdom, by which You created all things, might give suck to our souls' infancy. For I was not yet lowly enough to hold the lowly Jesus as my God, nor did I know what lesson His embracing of our weakness was to teach. For Your Word, the eternal Truth, towering above the highest parts of Your creation, lifts up to Himself those that were cast down. He built for Himself here below a lowly house of our clay, that by it He might bring down from themselves and bring up to Himself those who were to be made subject, healing the swollenness of their pride and fostering their love: so that their self-confidence might grow no further but rather diminish, seeing the deity at their feet, humbled by the assumption of our coat of human nature: to the end that weary at last they might cast themselves down upon His humanity and rise again in its rising.

O Lord, *I am Thy servant: I am Thy servant and the son of Thy handmaid. Thou has broken my bonds. I will sacrifice to Thee the sacrifice of praise.* Let my heart and my tongue praise Thee, and *let all my bones say, O Lord, who is like to Thee?* Let them say and do. Thou answer me and say to my soul: *I am Thy salvation.* Who am I and what kind of man am I? What evil has there not been in my deeds, or if not in my deeds, in my words, or if not in my words, then in my will? But You, Lord, are good and merciful, and Your right hand had regard to the profundity of my death and drew out the abyss of corruption that was in the bottom of my heart. By Your gift I had come totally not to will what I willed but to will what You willed. But where in all that long time was my free will, and from what deep sunken hiding-place was it suddenly summoned forth in the moment in which I bowed my neck to Your easy yoke and my shoulders to Your light burden, Christ Jesus, my Helper and my Redeemer?

How lovely I suddenly found it to be free from the loveliness of those vanities, so that now it was a joy to renounce what I had been so afraid to lose. For you cast them out of me, O true and supreme Loveliness, You cast them out of me and took their place in me. You who are sweeter than all pleasure, yet not to flesh and blood; brighter than all light, yet deeper within than any secret; loftier than all honour, but not to those who are lofty to themselves. Now my mind was free from the cares that had gnawed it, from aspiring and getting and weltering in filth and rubbing the scab of lust. And I talked with You as friends talk, my glory and my riches and my salvation, my Lord God.

The good I now sought was not in things outside me, to be seen by the eye of flesh under the sun. For those that find their joy outside them easily fall into emptiness and are spilled out upon the things that are seen and the things of time, and in their starved minds lick shadows. If only they could grow weary of their own hunger and say: *Who shall show us good things?* And we should say and they should hear: *The light of Thy countenance is sealed upon us,* O Lord. For we are not *the Light that enlightens every man* but we are enlightened by Thee that *as we were heretofore darkness we are now light in Thee.* If they could but see the Light interior and eternal: for now that I had known it, I was frantic that I could not make them see it even were they to ask: *Who shall show us good things?* For the heart they would bring me would be in their eyes, eyes that looked everywhere but at You. But there, where I had been angry with myself, in my own room where I had been pierced, where I had offered my sacrifice, slaying the self that I had been, and, in the newly-taken purpose of newness of life, hoping in You—there You began to make me feel Your love and to give *gladness in my heart.* I cried out as I read this aloud and realized it within: and I no longer wished any increase of earthly goods, in which a man wastes time and is wasted by time, since in the simplicity of the Eternal I had other corn and wine and oil.

Far be it, O Lord, far be it from the heart of Thy servant who makes this confession to Thee, far be it from me to think that I am happy for any or every joy that I may have. For there is a joy which is not given to the ungodly but only to those who love Thee for Thy own sake, whose joy is Thyself. And this is happiness, to be joyful in Thee and for Thee and because of Thee, this and no other. Those who think happiness is any other, pursue a joy that is apart from Thee and is no true joy. Yet their will is not wholly without some image of joy.

See now how great a space I have covered in my memory, in search of Thee, O Lord; and I have not found Thee outside it. For I find nothing concerning Thee but what I have remembered from the time I first learned of Thee. From that time, I have never forgotten Thee. For where I found truth, there I found my God, who is Truth Itself, and this I have not forgotten from the time I first learned it. Thus from the time I learned of Thee, Thou has remained in my memory, and there do I find Thee, when I turn my mind to Thee and find delight in Thee. These are my holy delights, which in Thy mercy Thou has given me, looking upon my poverty.

But where in my memory do You abide, Lord, where in my memory do You abide? What resting-place have You claimed as Your own, what sanctuary built for Yourself? You have paid this honour to my memory, that You deign to abide in it; but I now come to consider in what part of it You abide. In recalling You to mind I have mounted beyond those parts of memory which I have in common with the beasts, in that I did not find You among the images of corporeal things; and I came to those parts in which are kept the affections of my mind, and I could not find You there. And I came in to the innermost seat of my mind—which the mind has in my memory, since the mind remembers itself—and You were not there; because, just as You are not a corporeal image, or any affection of any living man such as we have when we are glad or sad, when we desire, fear, remember, forget and all such things: so You are not the mind itself, because You are the Lord God of the mind, and all these things suffer change, but You remain unchangeable over all: and yet You deign to dwell in my memory, ever since the time I first learned of You. And indeed why do I seek in what place of my memory You dwell as though there were places in my memory? Certain I am that You dwell in it, because I remember You since the time I first learned of You, and because I find You in it when I remember You.

Late have I loved Thee, O Beauty so ancient and so new; late have I loved Thee! For behold Thou wert within me, and I outside; and I sought Thee outside and in my unloveliness fell upon those lovely things that Thou hast made. Thou wert with me and I was not with Thee. I was kept from Thee by those things, yet had they not been in Thee, they would not have been at all. Thou didst call and cry to me and break open my deafness: and Thou didst send forth Thy beams and shine upon me and chase away my blindness: Thou didst breathe fragrance upon me, and I drew in my breath and do now pant for Thee: I tasted Thee, and now hunger and thirst for Thee: Thou didst touch me, and I have returned for Thy peace.

THE STEPS OF HUMILITY*
By Bernard, Abbot of Clairvaux

Of all medieval spiritual writers, St. Bernard is the most noted. He was the main spiritual force of the twelfth century. When he spoke, kings, popes and scholars listened. His Steps of Humility *is an important work of mystical literature by itself; it also influenced later literary works of mysticism. Herein Bernard gives his account of his mystical experience.*

THE STEPS OF HUMILITY
Bernard's own experience

Bernard himself had never had the experience of mystical contemplation when he wrote the letter to the Carthusians in 1125, for in this letter he denied the possibility of it. In *Loving God,* written probably in 1127, he repeated this letter without change; but in the new part of the essay he expressed his doubt of the possibility of mystical experience with more hesitation. In *Grace and Free Choice,* written in 1128, he asserted the possibility of it, but with an explicit emphasis which seems to indicate that he considered it a strange proposition which the reader would not naturally assume. In the *Steps of Humility,* written probably between 1129 and 1135, the possibility of mystical experience was taken for granted. In the 23rd sermon on Canticles, preached in 1137, he spoke of his own mystical experiences.

Toward the end of his life, in the 74th sermon on Canticles, he described his own experience in the following words:

I confess that the Word has come to me too *(I speak foolishly),* and many times. And although it has often entered me, I have never felt when it entered. I have felt that it was present, I remember that it was present, sometimes I could even anticipate its coming, but never feel it, nor its going either. For whence it came into my soul, or whither it went on leaving it again, even by what way it either came or went, I confess I know not even now; as it is said, *Thou canst not tell whence it cometh and whither it goeth.* And no wonder, for it is he to whom it was said, *Thy footsteps are not known.* Surely it came

*Copyright © 1940 by the President and Fellows of Howard College; revised 1968 by George B. Burch. Reprinted with permission, pp. 95-97.

not through the eyes, for it is colorless; nor through the ears, for it made no sound; nor through the nostrils, for it is not dissolved in the air, but in the mind—it created, rather than permeated, the air; nor through the mouth, for it is not chewed, or swallowed; nor have I discovered it by touch, for it is not palpable. By what way, then, has it entered? Or perhaps it did not enter at all, not having come from without? For it is not any of those things which are external. But neither has it come from within me, for it is good, and I know there is nothing good in me. I have ascended to that which is highest in me; and lo the Word rising above this. I have also descended through curiosity to explore what is lowest in me; and nevertheless it is found deeper still. If I have looked without, I have found it to be outside everything which is outside me; but if within, it was even more inward. And I have learned that it is true which I have read, that *in him we live and move and have our being;* but blessed is he in whom it is, who lives for it, who is moved by it.

Do you ask, then, since *his ways* are thus *past finding out,* how I know it is present? It *is quick and powerful;* and as soon as it entered, it awakened my sleeping soul; it moved, and softened, and wounded my heart, which was hard and stony and sick. It began also to root out and to pull down, to build and to plant, to water what was dry, enlighten what was dark, unlock what was closed, inflame what was cold, at the same time making *the crooked straight and the rough ways smooth,* so that *my soul* might *bless the Lord, and all that is within me bless his holy name.* And so it is that the Bridegroom Word, entering me at different times, has not made its entrance known by any signs, or voice, or appearance, or footstep. By no movement of its own is it manifested to me, by none of my senses does it penetrate within me; I have known its presence only by the beating of my heart, as I have just said, and I have discovered the power of its virtue by the expulsion of vices and the suppression of carnal emotions; and from the examination or reproof of my secret thoughts I have wondered at the profundity of its wisdom; and by any little improvement in my behavior I have experienced the goodness of its mercy; and by the renewal and reformation of the spirit of my mind, that is, of my inner man, I have perceived to some extent *the perfection of his beauty;* and from the contemplation of all these things together I have greatly feared *his excellent greatness.*

But when the Word has departed, just as if you should take

away the fire from beneath a boiling pot, all these things immediately begin to lie torpid and cold, in a sort of languor; and this is the sign of its withdrawal. Therefore my soul must be sad until it comes again, and my heart is warmed again within me, as it is wont; and this is the sign of the return.

THE FOUR DEGREES OF PASSIONATE LOVE*

By Richard of St. Victor

This passage is taken from *Mysticism: A Study and Anthology*
by F.C. Happold, London: Cox and Wyman, 1963.

*Another medieval author and contemporary of Bernard is
Richard of St. Victor (d. 1173), a prior of the abbey of St. Victor
in Paris. He was the first mystical writer to systematize
mystical theology. His approach is primarily psychological; he
was interested in the way rational and non-rational elements
combine in mystical states. To Richard the highest stage of the
mystical life is not one of selfish withdrawal from all concern
with the world, but is one in which a man, who has attained the
state of union, humbles himself and becomes the servant of his
fellow-men.*

THE FOUR DEGREES OF PASSIONATE LOVE

Let us go deeper and speak more openly. In the first degree
the soul thirsts for God, in the second she thirsts to go to God, in
the third she thirsts to be in God, in the fourth she thirsts in
God's way. She thirsts for God when she desires to experience
what that inward sweetness is that inebriates the mind of man,
when he begins to taste and see how sweet the Lord is. She
thirsts for God when she desires to be raised above herself by
the grace of contemplation and to see the Lord in all His
beauty, that she may truly say: 'For I have seen the Lord face to
face, and my life is preserved.' She thirsts in God, when in
ecstasy she desires to pass over into God altogether, so that
having wholly forgotten herself she may truly say: 'Whether in
the body or out of the body I cannot tell.' She thirsts in God's
way when, by her own will, I do not mean in temporal matters
only but also in spiritual things, the soul reserves nothing for
her own will but commits all things to God, never thinking
about herself but about the things of Jesus Christ, so that she
may say: 'I came not to do my own will but the will of the Father
which is in heaven.'

In the first degree, God enters into the soul and she turns
inward into herself. In the second, she ascends above herself

*Reprinted by permission of Faber and Faber, Ltd. from Richard of St. Victor: *Selected
Writings on Contemplation,* translated with an introduction and notes by Clare
Kirchberger, pp. 211-217.

and is lifted up to God. In the third the soul, lifted up to God, passes over altogether into Him. In the fourth the soul goes forth on God's behalf and descends below herself. In the first she enters into herself, in the second she goes forth from herself. In the first she reaches her own life, in the third she reaches God. In the first she goes forth on her own behalf, in the fourth she goes forth because of her neighbour. In the first she enters in by meditation, in the second she ascends by contemplation, in the third she is led into jubilation, in the fourth she goes out by compassion.

In the first degree, spiritual feeling sweeter than honey enters into her soul and inebriates her with its sweetness, so that she has honey and milk on her tongue and her lips distil the honeycomb. Those who have felt this will give forth a memorial of abundant sweetness, for the mouth speaketh out of the abundance of the heart. This is the first consolation which they who renounce the world receive at first and it generally confirms them in their good intention. This is the heavenly food which is wont to refresh those who go forth from Egypt and to feed them in the wilderness; this is the hidden manna which no man knoweth who hath not received it . . . .

But first we must leave Egypt[112] behind, first we must cross the Red Sea. First the Egyptians must perish in the waves, first we must suffer famine in the land of Egypt before we can receive this spiritual nourishment and heavenly food. He who desires that food of heavenly solitude let him abandon Egypt both in body and heart, and altogether set aside the love of the world. Let him cross the Red Sea, let him try to drive all sadness and bitterness out of his heart, if he desires to be filled with inward sweetness. First the Egyptians must be swallowed up. Let perverse ways perish lest the angelic citizens disdain an ignoble companion. First the foods of Egypt must fail, and carnal pleasures be held in abomination before we may experience the nature of those inner and eternal pleasures.

In this state the Lord often visits the hungry and thirsty soul, often He fills her with inward delight and makes her drink with the sweetness of His spirit. Nevertheless He reveals His presence but without showing His face. He infuses His sweetness but does not show His fair beauty. His loveliness is felt but

---

112. Egypt was commonly used as the symbol of the material world (cf. *The Hymn of the Robe of Glory,* pages 176-81). As the Israelites had to leave Egypt and endure the rigours of the desert of Sinai before reaching the Promised Land, so the soul must shake off the shackles of the material in order that it may find the Heavenly City.

His form is not discerned. Even now the clouds and darkness are round about Him and His throne is in the pillar of the cloud. Gentle and soothing is that which is felt, but altogether dark, what is seen. For He does not yet appear in the light, and though He be seen in the fire, the fire is a burning rather than an illumination. For He kindles the affection but does not yet illuminate the intellect. He inflames the desire but does not yet enlighten the intelligence. In this state the soul can feel her beloved but she cannot see Him. And if she does see Him it is as one sees by night. She sees as it were in a cloud, she sees Him at last in a mirror and darkly, not yet face to face.

At times [the mind] begins to be more bold and to ask for higher things. Nevertheless it does not receive immediately what it asks, nor according to its desire, though it may ask with deep desire. But knowing that he who asketh receiveth, who seeketh findeth, and that the door is opened to him that knocketh, again and again he is given confidence and his strength is renewed and he says: 'My face hath sought Thee. Thy face, O Lord, will I seek.' When the mind therefore goes forward to the grace of contemplation with great effort and ardent desire, it moves as it were into the second degree of love, where it deserves to look, by divine shewing, upon that which the eye cannot see nor the ear hear nor shall it enter the heart of man, so that it may truly say: 'But to us, God hath revealed them by His spirit.'

The shewing of the divine light in this state and the wonder of the revelation arising from it, together with the perennial memory thereof bind the soul indissolubly so that she is not able to forget the happiness of her experience. And as in the earlier degree, the delight which she has tasted satisfied the soul and transfixes the affections, so in this degree, the brightness she has looked upon binds the thoughts that she may neither forget it nor think about anything else.

The third degree of love is when the mind of man is ravished into the abyss of divine light so that the soul, having forgotten all outward things, is altogether unaware of itself and passes out completely into its God. In this state it is wholly subdued, the host of carnal desires are deeply asleep and there is silence in heaven as it were for half an hour. And any suffering that is left is absorbed in glory. In this state, while the soul is abstracted from itself, ravished into that secret place of divine refuge, when it is surrounded on every side by the divine fire of love, pierced to the core, set alight all about, then it sheds its very self altogether and puts on that divine life, and being wholly conformed to the beauty it has seen passes wholly into that glory . . . .

As soon as she is admitted to that inner secret of the divine mystery, through the greatness of her wonder and the abundance of joy, she is wholly dissolved in herself, or rather into Him who speaks, when she begins to hear words that it is not lawful for man to utter and to understand the strange and hidden things of God. In this state she who cleaves to the Lord is one spirit with him. In this state, as we have said, the soul is altogether melted into him whom she loves and is herself fainting away . . . .

Similarly those who have reached the third degree of love, do nothing according to their own will, they leave nothing at their own desire, but commit all things to the providence of God. Every wish or desire of theirs hangs upon God's sign and awaits the divine good pleasure. And as the first degree wounds the affection and the second binds the thoughts, so the third hinders action, so that a man cannot be occupied about anything unless the power of the divine will draws or drives him. When in this way the soul has been reduced in the divine fire, softened to the very core and wholly melted, nothing is wanting except that she should be shown what is God's good will, all pleasing and perfect, even the form of perfect virtue, to which she must be conformed. For just as the metal workers, when the metals are melted and the moulds set out, shape any form according to their will and produce any vessel according to the manner and mould that has been planned, so the soul applies herself in this degree, to be readily at the beck and call of the divine will, indeed she adapts herself with spontaneous desire to every demand of God and adjusts her own will, as the divine good pleasure requires. And as liquefied metal runs down easily wherever a passage is opened, so the soul humbles herself spontaneously to be obedient in this way, and freely bows herself in all acts of humility according to the order of divine providence.

In this state the image of the will of Christ is set before the soul so that these words come to her: 'Let this mind be in you, which was also in Christ Jesus: who being in the form of God, thought it not robbery to be equal with God, but emptied himself, and took upon him the form of a servant, and was made in the likeness of men, and was found in the habit of man; he humbled himself and became obedient unto death, even the death of the cross.' This is the form of the humility of Christ to which every man must conform himself, who desires to attain to the highest degree of perfect charity. For greater love has no man than this, that a man lay down his life for his friends. Those who are able to lay down their lives for their friends have reached the highest peak of charity and are already placed in the fourth degree of charity. They can fulfil the Apostle's bidding: 'Be ye therefore followers of God, as dear children: and walk in love, as Christ also hath loved us, and hath given himself for an offering and a sacrifice to God for a sweetsmelling savour.'

Therefore in the third degree the soul is glorified, in the fourth she is humbled for God's sake. In the third she is conformed to the divine light, in the fourth she is humbled for God's sake. In the third she is conformed to the divine light, in the fourth she is conformed to the humility of Christ. And though in the third she is in a way almost in the likeness of God, nevertheless in the fourth she begins to empty herself, taking the form of a servant, and begins to be found in fashion as a man. In the third degree she is as it were put to death in God, in the fourth she is raised in Christ. He that is in the fourth degree may say truly: 'I live yet not I, Christ liveth in me.' Such a man begins to live in newness of life, and for the rest, 'to him to live is Christ and to die gain.' He is truly in a strait between two desires, to be dissolved and be with Christ which is far better, but to remain in the flesh is necessary for our sakes. The charity of Christ compels him. Such a man becomes a new creature, for old things are passed away and lo! all things are made new. For in the third degree he is put to death, in the fourth, as it were, he rises from the dead, now he dieth no more, death hath no more dominion over him, for in that he liveth he liveth unto God.

Therefore, in the fourth degree, the soul is made in some way immortal and impassible. How can it be mortal if it cannot die? and how can it die if it cannot be separated from Him who is life? We know who said this: 'I am the way, the truth, and the life.' How then can a man die who cannot be separated from Him? 'For I am sure,' he saith, 'that neither death, nor life, nor angels, nor principalities, nor powers, nor things present, nor things to come, nor might, nor height, nor depth, nor any other creature, shall be able to separate us from the love of God which is' in Christ Jesus.' Besides, does a man not seem, in some degree, impassible, who does not feel the misfortunes that he bears, who rejoices in injuries, and whatever pain he suffers he counts it to be glory? according to the saying of the Apostle: 'Gladly therefore I will glory in my infirmities that the power of Christ may dwell in me.' He who takes pleasure in sufferings and contumely for Christ, also seems to be impassible. 'Therefore, I take pleasure in infirmities, in reproaches, in necessities, in persecutions, in distresses for Christ's sake.' He who is in this degree can say confidently: 'I can do all things in him who strengthened me,' in that he knows how to be filled and how to be hungry, to abound and to suffer poverty. In this degree of charity he 'beareth all things, believeth all things, hopeth all things, endureth all things.' In this degree charity is long-suffering and is kind, is not ambitious, seeketh not her own, does not render evil for evil nor curse for a curse. But rather blesseth. He who ascends to this degree of charity is truly in the state of love that can say: 'I am made all things to all men that I might save all.' And such a man then desires to be made anathema from Christ for his brethren's sake. What shall we say then? In this degree of love the soul of man might seem to be mad, in that it will not suffer his zeal to be kept within bounds or measure. Is it not complete madness to reject true life, to accuse the highest wisdom, to resist omnipotence? And if a man desires to be separated from Christ for his brethren's sake, is that not a rejection of true life? . . . Consider to what boldness of presumption the perfection of charity can raise up the mind of man: behold how it induces him to presume beyond the power of a man! That which he hopes of God, what he does for God and in God and effects with God, is more than merely human. How utterly wondrous and amazing! The more he hopes from God the more he abases himself for God. The more he rises up in boldness, the more he descends in humility. Just as the goal to which he ascends by confidence is above man, so is the point to which he descends by patience, beyond man.

Therefore as we have said, in the first degree, the soul returns to itself; in the second it ascends to God; in the third it passes out into God; in the fourth it descends below itself. In the first and second it is raised; in the third and fourth it is transfigured. In the first it ascends to itself; in the second it transcends itself; in the third it is conformed to the glory of Christ; in the fourth it is conformed to the humility of Christ. Again, in the first it is led back; in the second it is transferred; in the third it is transformed; in the fourth it is resurrected.

INTERIOR CASTLE*
By St. Teresa of Avila
Trans. and edited by E. Allison Peers

Teresa needs no further introduction. Notice, however, the various kinds of spiritual states that she experiences. She is a master of description. Her experiences in these readings are much more intense than in the simple union previously read.

INTERIOR CASTLE
Treats of occasions when God suspends the soul in prayer by means of rapture, or ecstasy, or trance (for I think these are all the same), and of how great courage is necessary if we are to receive great favours from His Majesty.

How much rest can this poor little butterfly have amid all these trials and other things that I have described? Its whole will is set on desiring to have ever-increasing fruition of its Spouse; and His Majesty, knowing our weakness, continues to grant it the things it wants, and many more, so that it may have the courage to achieve union with so great a Lord and to take Him for its Spouse.

You will laugh at my saying this and call it ridiculous, for you will all think courage is quite unnecessary and suppose there is no woman, however lowly, who would not be brave enough to betroth herself to the King. This would be so, I think, with an earthly king, but for betrothal with the King of Heaven I must warn you that there is more need of courage than you imagine, because our nature is very timid and lowly for so great an undertaking, and I am certain that, unless God granted us strength,[113] it would be impossible. And now you are going to see what His Majesty does to confirm this betrothal, for this, as

---

*Reprinted from *The Interior Castle* by St. Teresa of Avila in *The Complete Works of St. Teresa*, trans. and ed. by E. Allison Peers from the critical edition of P. Silverio De Santa Teresa, O.C.D., published in three volumes by Sheed and Ward, Inc., New York. Excerpt from Image Books, 1961, pp. 148-162.

113. [The original here interpolates two clauses, *con cuanto veis, u que nos esta bien*, which, translated literally as "with all that you see or that it is acceptable to us," make no sense. I suspect that, if St. Teresa had re-read her words, the phrase would have been omitted or clarified. Freely it might be rendered: "wonderful as you see it to be and much as we appreciate it," or, "however many visions you see or however much we desire them," but I am not convinced that either of these translations represents the author's meaning and other paraphrases are admissible.]

I understand it, is what happens when He bestows raptures, which carry the soul out of its senses; for if, while still in possession of its senses, the soul saw that it was so near to such great majesty, it might perhaps be unable to remain alive. It must be understood that I am referring to genuine raptures, and not to women's weaknesses, which we all have in this life, so that we are apt to think everything is rapture and ecstasy. And, as I believe I have said, there are some people who have such poor constitutions that one experience of the Prayer of Quiet kills them. I want to enumerate here some different kinds of rapture which I have got to know about through conversations with spiritual people. I am not sure if I shall succeed in doing so, any more than when I wrote of this before.[114] For various reasons it has been thought immaterial if I should repeat myself in discussing this and other matters connected with it, if for no other object than that of setting down in one place all that there is to be said about each Mansion.

One kind of rapture is this. The soul, though not actually engaged in prayer, is struck by some word, which it either remembers or hears spoken by God. His Majesty is moved with compassion at having seen the soul suffering so long through its yearning for Him, and seems to be causing the spark of which we have already spoken to grow within it, so that, like the phoenix, it catches fire and springs into new life. One may piously believe that the sins of such a soul are pardoned, assuming that it is in the proper disposition and has used the means of grace, as the Church teaches.[115] When it is thus cleansed, God unites it with Himself, in a way which none can understand save it and He, and even the soul itself does not understand this in such a way as to be able to speak of it afterwards, though it is not deprived of its interior senses; for it is not like one who suffers a swoon or a paroxysm so that it can understand nothing either within itself or without.

The position, in this case, as I understand it, is that the soul has never before been so fully awake to the things of God or had such light or such knowledge of His Majesty. This may seem impossible; because, if the faculties are so completely absorbed that we might describe them as dead, and the senses are so as well, how can the soul be said to understand this secret? I

114. *Life,* Chap. XX; *Relations,* V.
115. The phrase "assuming ... teaches" was added by St. Teresa, in the autograph, as a marginal note.

cannot say, nor perhaps can any creature, but only the Creator Himself, nor can I speak of many other things that happen in this state—I mean in these two Mansions, for this and the last might be fused in one: there is no closed door to separate the one from the other. As, however, there are things in the latter Mansion which are not shown to those who have not yet reached it, I have thought it best to separate them.

When the soul is in this state of suspension and the Lord sees fit to reveal to it certain mysteries, such as heavenly things and imaginary visions, it is able subsequently to describe these, for they are so deeply impressed upon the memory that they can never again be forgotten. But when they are intellectual visions they cannot be so described; for at these times come visions of so sublime a kind that it is not fitting for those who live on earth to understand them in such a way that they can describe them; although after regaining possession of their senses they can often describe many of these intellectual visions.

It may be that some of you do not understand what is meant by a vision, especially by an intellectual vision. I shall explain this in due course, as I have been commanded to do so by him who has authority over me; and although it may seem irrelevant there may possibly be souls who will find it helpful. "But," you will say to me, "if the soul is not going to remember these sublime favours which the Lord grants it in this state, how can they bring it any profit?" Oh, daughters, the profit is so great that it cannot be exaggerated, for, although one cannot describe these favours, they are clearly imprinted in the very depths of the soul and they are never forgotten. "But," you will say next, "if the soul retains no image of them and the faculties are unable to understand them, how can they be remembered?" This, too, is more than I can understand; but I know that certain truths concerning the greatness of God remains so firmly in the soul that even had it not faith which will tell it Who He is and that it is bound to believe Him to be God, the soul would adore Him as such from that very moment, just as Jacob adored Him when he saw the ladder.[116] He must, of course, have learned other secrets which he could not describe; for, if he had not had more interior light, he would not have understood such great mysteries merely from seeing a ladder on which angels were descending and ascending.

116. Genesis xxviii, 12.

I do not know if I am right in what I am saying, for, although I have heard of the incident, I am not sure if I remember it correctly. Moses, again, could not describe all that he saw in the bush, but only as much as God willed him to,[117] yet, if God had not revealed secret things to his soul in such a way as to make him sure of their truth, so that he should know and believe Him to be God, he would not have taken upon himself so many and such arduous labours. Amid the thorns of that bush he must have learned marvellous things, for it was these things which gave him courage to do what he did for the people of Israel. Therefore, sisters, we must not seek out reasons for understanding the hidden things of God; rather, believing, as we do, in His great power, we must clearly realize that it is impossible for worms like ourselves, with our limited powers, to understand His greatness. Let us give Him hearty praise for being pleased to allow us to understand some part of it.

I am wishing I could find a suitable comparison which would give some sort of explanation of what I am saying. But I can think of none that will answer my purpose. Let us put it like this, however. You enter a private apartment in the palace of a king or a great lord (I think they call it a *camarin)*, where they have an infinite variety of glassware, and earthenware, and all kinds of things, set out in such a way that you can see almost all of them as you enter. I was once taken into a room of this kind in the house of the Duchess of Alba, where I was commanded by obedience to stay,[118] in the course of a journey, at her pressing invitation. When I went in I was astounded and began to wonder what all this mass of things could be used for, and then I realized that the sight of so many different things might lead one to glorify the Lord. It occurs to me now how useful an experience it was for my present purpose. Although I was there for some time, there was so much to be seen that I could not remember it all, so that I could no more recall what was in those rooms than if I had never seen them, nor could I say what the things were made of; I can only remember having seen them as a whole.[119] It is just like that here. The soul becomes one with God. It is brought into this mansion of the empyrean Heaven which we must have in the depths of our

---

117. Exodus iii, 2.
118. "Two days," adds the *editio princeps*. The visit was made at the beginning of 1574; see "Outline, etc.," Vol. I, p. xxxi, above.
119. The sentence "I can . . . whole" was written by St. Teresa in the margin of the autograph.

souls; for it is clear that, since God dwells in them, He must have one[120] of these mansions. And although while the soul is in ecstasy the Lord will not always wish it to see these secrets (for it is so much absorbed in its fruition of Him that the great blessing suffices it). He is sometimes pleased that it should emerge from its absorption, and then it will at once see what there is in this room; in which case, after coming to itself, it will remember that revelation of the great things it has seen. It will not, however, be able to describe any of them, nor will its nature be able to apprehend more of the supernatural than God has been pleased to reveal to it.

Is this tantamount to an admission on my part that is has really seen something and that this is an imaginary vision? I do not mean that at all, for it is not of imaginary, but of intellectual visions that I am treating; only I have no learning and am too stupid to explain anything; and I am quite clear that, if what I have said so far about this kind of prayer is put correctly, it is not I who have said it. My own belief is that, if the soul to whom God has given these secrets in its raptures never understands any of them, they proceed, not from raptures at all, but from some natural weakness, which is apt to affect people of feeble constitution, such as women. In such cases the spirit, by making a certain effort, can overcome nature and remain in a state of absorption, as I believe I said when dealing with the Prayer of Quiet. Such experiences as these have nothing to do with raptures; for when a person is enraptured you can be sure that God is taking her entire soul to Himself, and that, as she is His own property and has now become His bride, He is showing her some little part of the kingdom which she has gained by becoming so. This part may be only a small one, but everything that is in this great God is very great. He will not allow her to be disturbed either by the faculties or by the senses; so He at once commands that all the doors of these Mansions shall be shut, and only the door of the Mansion in which He dwells remains open so that we may enter. Blessed be such great mercy! Rightly shall those who will not profit by it, and who thus forgo the presence of their Lord, be called accursed.

Oh, my sisters, what nothingness is all that we have given up, and all that we are doing, or can ever do, for a God Who is

120. [Or "some": the Spanish word, *alguna,* can have either a singular or a plural sense.]

pleased to communicate Himself in this way to a worm! If we have the hope of enjoying this blessing while we are still in this life, what are we doing about it and why are we waiting? What sufficient reason is there for delaying even a short time instead of seeking this Lord, as the Bride did, through streets and squares?[121] Oh, what a mockery is everything in the world if it does not lead us and help us on the way towards this end,—and would be even though all the worldly delights and riches and joys that we can imagine were to last for ever! For everything is cloying and degrading by comparison with these treasures, which we shall enjoy eternally. And even these are nothing by comparison with having for our own the Lord of all treasures and of Heaven and earth.

Oh, human blindness! How long, how long shall it be before this dust is removed from our eyes? For although, as far as we ourselves are concerned, it seems not to be bad enough to blind us altogether, I can see some motes and particles which, if we allow them to become more numerous, will be sufficient to do us great harm. For the love of God, then, sisters, let us profit by these faults and learn from them what wretched creatures we are, and may they give us clearer sight, as did the clay to the blind man who was healed by our Spouse;[122] and thus, realizing our own imperfections, we shall beseech Him more and more earnestly to bring good out of our wretchedness, so that we may please His Majesty in everything.

Without realizing it, I have strayed far from my theme. Forgive me, sisters; and believe me, now that I have come to these great things of God (come to write about them, I mean), I cannot help feeling the pity of it when I see how much we are losing, and all through our own fault. For, true though it is that these are things which the Lord gives to whom He will, he would give them to us all if we loved Him as He loves us. For He desires nothing else but to have those to whom He may give them, and His riches are not diminished by His readiness to give.

Returning now to what I was saying, the Spouse orders the doors of the Mansions to be shut, and even those of the Castle and its enclosure. For when He means to enrapture this soul, it loses its power of breathing, with the result that, although its other senses sometimes remain active a little longer, it cannot

---

121. [The "streets and the broad ways" of Canticles iii, 2.]
122. St. John ix, 6-7.

possibly speak. At other times it loses all its powers at once, and the hands and the body grow so cold that the body seems no longer to have a soul—sometimes it even seems doubtful if there is any breath in the body. This lasts only for a short time (I mean, only for a short period at any one time) because, when this profound suspension lifts a little, the body seems to come partly to itself again, and draws breath, though only to die once more, and, in doing so, to give fuller life to the soul. Complete ecstasy, therefore, does not last long.

But, although relief comes, the ecstasy has the effect of leaving the will so completely absorbed and the understanding so completely transported—for as long as a day, or even for several days—that the soul seems incapable of grasping anything that does not awaken the will to love; to this it is fully awake, while asleep as regards all that concerns attachment to any creature.

Oh, what confusion the soul feels when it comes to itself again and what ardent desires it has to be used for God in any and every way in which He may be pleased to employ it! If such effects as have been described result from the former kinds of prayer, what can be said of a favour as great as this? Such a soul would gladly have a thousand lives so as to use them all for God, and it would like everything on earth to be tongue so that it might praise Him. It has tremendous desires to do penance; and whatever penance it does it counts as very little, for its love is so strong that it feels everything it does to be of very small account and realizes clearly that it was not such a great matter for the martyrs to suffer all their tortures, for with the aid of Our Lord such a thing becomes easy. And thus these souls make complaint to Our Lord when He offers them no means of suffering.

When this favour is granted them secretly they esteem it very highly; for so great are the shame and the confusion caused them by having to suffer before others that to some extent they lessen the soul's absorption in what it was enjoying, because of the distress and the anxiety which arise from its thoughts of what others who have seen it will think. For, knowing the malice of the world, they realize that their suffering may perhaps not be attributed to its proper cause but may be made an occasion for criticism instead of for glorifying the Lord. This distress and shame are no longer within the soul's own power of control, yet they seem to me to denote a lack of humility; for if such a person really desires to be despitefully treated, how can she mind if she is? One who is distressed in this way heard Our Lord say: "Be not afflicted, for either they will praise Me or murmur at thee, and in either case thou wilt be the gainer."[123] I learned afterwards that that person had been greatly cheered and consoled by those words; and I set them down here for the sake of any who find themselves in this affliction. It seems that Our Lord wants everyone to realize that such a person's soul is now His and that no one must touch it. People are welcome to attack her body, her honour, and her possessions, for any of these attacks will be to His Majesty's honour. But her soul they may not attack, for unless, with most blameworthy presumption, it tears itself away from its Spouse, He will protect it from the whole world, and indeed from all hell.

I do not know if I have conveyed any impression of the nature of rapture: to give a full idea of it, as I have said, is impossible. Still, I think there has been no harm in my saying this, so that its nature may be understood, since the effects of feigned raptures are so different. (I do not use the word "feigned" because those who experience them wish to deceive, but because they are deceived themselves.)[124] As the signs and effects of these last do not harmonize with the reception of this great favour, the favour itself becomes discredited, so that those to whom the Lord grants it later on are not believed. May He be for ever blessed and praised. Amen. Amen.

Continues the same subject and gives an example of how God exalts the soul through flights of the spirit in a way different from that described. Gives some reasons why courage is necessary here. Says something of this favour which God grants in a way so delectable. This chapter is highly profitable.

There is another kind of rapture, or flight of the spirit, as I call it, which, though substantially the same, is felt within the soul[125] in a very different way. Sometimes the soul becomes

123. Cf. *Life*, Chap. XXXI [Image Books Edition, 292].
124. This is Luis de León's emendation of the sentence in the autograph, which reads: "I do not use the word 'feigned,' because those who experience them do not wish to deceive, but because [*sic*] they are deceived themselves." Gracian in the Cordoba copy, emends similarly, though not identically. Both evidently express what St. Teresa meant but failed to put clearly.
125. The mystics concur with St. Thomas in holding that ecstasy, rapture, transport, flight of the spirit, etc., are in substance one and the same, though there are accidental differences between them, as St. Teresa explains here, in *Life*, Chap. XX, and in *Relations*, V.

conscious of such rapid motion that the spirit seems to be transported with a speed which, especially at first, fills it with fear, for which reason I told you that great courage is necessary for anyone in whom God is to work these favours, together with faith and confidence and great resignation, so that Our Lord may do with the soul as He wills. Do you suppose it causes but little perturbation to a person in complete possession of his senses when he experiences these transports of the soul? We have even read in some authors that the body is transported as well as the soul without knowing whither it is going, or who is bearing it away, or how, for when this sudden motion begins the soul has no certainty that it is caused by God.

Can any means of resisting this be found? None whatever: on the contrary, resistance only makes matters worse. This I know from a certain person who said that God's will seems to be to show the soul that, since it has so often and so unconditionally placed itself in His hands, and has offered itself to Him with such complete willingness, it must realize that it is no longer its own mistress, and so the violence with which it is transported becomes markedly greater. This person, therefore, decided to offer no more resistance than a straw does when it is lifted up by amber (if you have ever observed this) and to commit herself into the hands of Him Who is so powerful, seeing that it is but to make a virtue of necessity. And, speaking of straw, it is a fact that a powerful man cannot bear away a straw more easily than this great and powerful Giant of ours can bear away the spirit.

I think that basin of water, of which we spoke in (I believe) the fourth Mansion (but I do not remember exactly where),[126] was being filled at that stage gently and quietly—I mean without any movement. But now this great God, Who controls the sources of the waters and forbids the sea to move beyond its bounds, has loosed the sources whence water has been coming into this basin; and with tremendous force there rises up so powerful a wave that this little ship—our soul—is lifted up on high. And if a ship can do nothing, and neither the pilot nor any of the crew has any power over it, when the waves make a furious assault upon it and toss it about at their will, even less able is the interior part of the soul to stop where it likes, while its senses and faculties can do no more than has been commanded them: the exterior senses, however, are quite unaffected by this.

126. IV, ii [p. 80, above].

Really, sisters, the mere writing of this makes me astounded when I reflect how the great power of this great King and Emperor manifests itself here. What, then, must be the feelings of anyone who experiences it? For my own part I believe that, if His Majesty were to reveal Himself to those who journey through the world to their perdition as He does to these souls, they would not dare—out of very fear, though not perhaps out of love—to offend Him. Oh, how great, then, are the obligations attending souls who have been warned in so sublime a way to strive with all their might so as not to offend this Lord! For His sake, sisters, I beseech you, to whom His Majesty has granted these favours or others like them, not merely to receive them and then grow careless, but to remember that anyone who owes much has much to pay.[127]

This is another reason why the soul needs great courage, for the thought is one which makes it very fearful, and, did Our Lord not give it courage, it would continually be in great affliction. When it reflects what His Majesty is doing with it, and then turns to reflect upon itself, it realizes what a little it is doing towards the fulfillment of its obligations and how feeble is that little which it does do and how full of faults and failures. If it does any good action, rather than remember how imperfect this action is, it thinks best to try to forget it, to keep nothing in mind but its sins, and to throw itself upon the mercy of God; and, since it has, nothing with which to pay, it craves the compassion and mercy which He has always shown to sinners.

He may perhaps answer it as He answered someone who was very much distressed about this, and was looking at a crucifix and thinking that she had never had anything to offer God or to give up for His sake. The Crucified Himself comforted her by saying that He was giving her all the pains and trials which He had suffered in His Passion, so that she should have them for her own to offer to His Father.[128] That soul, as I have understood from her, was so much comforted and enriched by this experience that she cannot forget it, and, whenever she feels miserable, she remembers it and it comforts and encourages her. There are several other remarks on this subject which I might add; for, as I have had to do with many saintly and prayerful people, I know of a number of such cases, but I do

---

127. St. Luke xii, 28.
128. St. Teresa received this favour at Seville about 1575-6. Cf. *Relations*, LI (Vol. I, *The Complete Works of St. Teresa*, p. 360.)

not want you to think that it is to myself that I am referring, so I pass them over. This incident which I have described seems to me a very apt one for helping you to understand how glad Our Lord is when we get to know ourselves and keep trying all the time to realize our poverty and wretchedness, and to reflect that we possess nothing that we have not been given. Therefore, my sisters, courage is necessary for this and for many other things that happen to a soul which the Lord has brought to this state; and, to my thinking, if the soul is humble, more courage is necessary for this last state than for any other. May the Lord, of His own bounty, grant us humility.

Turning now to this sudden transport of the spirit, it may be said to be of such a kind that the soul really seems to have left the body; on the other hand, it is clear that the person is not dead, though for a few moments he cannot even himself be sure if the soul is in the body or no. He feels as if he has been in another world, very different from this in which we live, and has been shown a fresh light there, so much unlike any to be found in this life that, if he had been imagining it, and similar things, all his life long, it would have been impossible for him to obtain any idea of them. In a single instant he is taught so many things all at once that, if he were to labour for years on end in trying to fit them all into his imagination and thought, he could not succeed with a thousandth part of them. This is not an intellectual, but an imaginary vision, which is seen with the eyes of the soul very much more clearly than we can ordinarily see things with the eyes of the body; and some of the revelations are communicated to it without some words. If, for example, he sees any of the saints, he knows them as well as if he had spent a long time in their company.

Sometimes, in addition to the things which he sees with the eyes of the soul, in intellectual vision, others are revealed to him—in particular, a host of angels, with their Lord; and, though he sees nothing with the eyes of the body or with the eyes of the soul, he is shown the things I am describing, and many others which are indescribable, by means of an admirable kind of knowledge. Anyone who has experience of this, and possesses more ability than I, will perhaps know how to express it; to me it seems extremely difficult. If the soul is in the body or not while all this is happening I cannot say; I would not myself swear that the soul is in the body, nor that the body is bereft of the soul.

I have often thought that if the sun can remain in the heavens and yet its rays are so strong that without its moving thence they can none the less reach us here, it must be possible for the soul and the spirit, which are as much the same thing as are the sun and its rays, to remain where they are, and yet, through the power of the heat that comes to them from the true Sun of Justice, for some higher part of them to rise above itself. Really, I hardly know what I am saying; but it is a fact that, as quickly as a bullet leaves a gun when the trigger is pulled, there begins within the soul a flight (I know no other name to give it) which, though no sound is made, is so clearly a movement that it cannot possibly be due to fancy. When the soul, as far as it can understand, is right outside itself, great things are revealed to it; and, when it returns to itself, it finds that it has reaped very great advantages and it has such contempt for earthly things that, in comparison with those it has seen, they seem like dirt to it. Thenceforward to live on earth is a great affliction to it, and, if it sees any of the things which used to give it pleasure, it no longer cares for them. Just as tokens of the nature of the Promised Land were brought back by those whom the Israelites sent on there,[129] so in this case the Lord's wish seems to have been to show the soul something of the country to which it is to travel, so that it may suffer the trials of this trying road,[130] knowing whither it must travel in order to obtain its rest. Although you may think that a thing which passes so quickly cannot be of great profit, the help which it gives the soul is so great that only the person familiar with it can understand its worth.

Clearly, then, this is no work of the devil; such an experience could not possibly proceed from the imagination, and the devil could never reveal things which produce such results in the soul and leave it with such peace and tranquillity and with so many benefits. There are three things in particular which it enjoys to a very high degree. The first is knowledge of the greatness of God: the more we see of this, the more deeply we are conscious of it. The second is self-knowledge and humility at realizing how a thing like the soul, so base by comparison with One Who is the Creator of such greatness, has dared to offend Him and dares to raise its eyes to Him. The third is a supreme contempt for earthly things, save those which can be

129. Numbers xiii, 18-24.
130. [*Los trabajos de este camino tan trabajoso:* the word-play is intentional.]

employed in the service of so great a God.

These are the jewels which the Spouse is beginning to give to His bride, and so precious are they that she will not fail to keep them with the greatest care. These meetings[131] with the Spouse remain so deeply engraven in the memory that I think it is impossible for the soul to forget them until it is enjoying them for ever; if it did so, it would suffer the greatest harm. But the Spouse Who gives them to the soul has power also to give it grace not to lose them.

Returning now to the soul's need of courage, I ask you: Does it seem to you such a trifling thing after all? For the soul really feels that it is leaving the body when it sees the senses leaving it and has no idea why they are going. So He Who gives everything else must needs give courage too. You will say that this fear of the soul's is well rewarded; so too say I. May He Who can give so much be for ever praised. And may it please His Majesty to grant us to be worthy to serve Him. Amen.

131. [*Vistas.* Cf. p. 119, above.]

THE SEVEN STEPS OF THE LADDER
OF SPIRITUAL LOVE*
By John Ruysbroeck

Some authors believe John Ruysbroeck (1293-1381) is the greatest mystic of the church. Ruysbroeck, a priest in Flanders, always treats the spiritual life as a growth or progress. Only those whose will and senses have been mortified are prepared to receive the gift of mystical union. The deeper one grows, Ruysbroeck believes, the greater outward charity and inward peace he will have.

THE SEVENTH STEP
THE CONTEMPLATIVE LIFE IN ITS SECOND
MOMENT. THE ANNIHILATION IN GOD'S ESSENCE

Here follows the seventh and last step, the most excellent and highest which can be realised either in time or in eternity. It comes about, when above all conception and knowledge we find in ourselves a certain infinite or abyssal unknowing; when, transcending every name which has been given to God or to any created thing, we expire into the eternal nameless-ness, wherein we are lost; when, beyond any practice of virtue we contemplate and find within us an eternal repose, in which no man can work; and, above all blessed spirits, a blessedness without measure, in which we are all one, and that same one which is that blessedness itself in its essence; and when at length we contemplate all blessed spirits as in essence drowned and melted and lost in the supersubstantial essence, in a path-less unknown darkness.

The distinction between God and Godhead as the groundwork for the second moment

We will also contemplate the Father and Son and Holy Ghost, Trinity in Persons, one God in nature, Creator of heaven and earth and all that exists: Whom we will love, and thank, and praise eternally. He made us to His image and likeness, which is great joy to pure and excellent minds. His Godhead indeed does not work, since it is a simple essence at rest: and if we possessed that rest with God, we should be rest itself with Him, and should have risen to His loftiness and, beyond all steps of the heavenly ladder, have become with Him in his

*Reprinted by permission of Adam and Charles Black Publishers, London, England, pp. 57-63.

Godhead an essence in repose and an eternal blessedness. The divine Persons in the fecundity of Their nature are one God eternally in action, and in the simplicity of Their essence, they are Godhead, perpetual rest; and so with respect to His Persons, God is an eternal operation, but with respect to His essence, eternal rest.

The love of God in operation, and the ceasing from His service corresponding to the aforesaid distinction

Furthermore between action and rest live love and fruition. Love would ever be at work since it is an everlasting inter-action with God; but fruition must ever be at rest, above all will or desire, the embracing of the well-beloved in the well-beloved, in a love pure and without images. Therein the Father together with His Son clasps His beloved in the restful unity of His Spirit, above the fecundity of His nature; and to each single spirit He says with eternal well-pleasedness, 'I belong to you, and you to Me: I am yours and you are Mine; I have chosen you from eternity.' Whereat, so great is the mutual joy and delight between God and His beloved spirits, that they are rapt out of themselves and melt and flow to become one spirit with God in fruition, being drawn eternally into the abyssal blessedness of His essence. And this is the first form of fruition in the contemplation of living men.

God's touch or inbreathing as a way in the inner life to the annihilation of the contemplative in God

There is yet a second way which brings to the fruition of God inward and devoted men, made perfect in charity according to His dearest will. It is for such as deny themselves, abandon themselves and shun everything that could be possessed with delight and love, and everything created by God which could be a source of care and hindrance in that inner life wherein they serve Him. Thereby they are raised up towards God with loving affection coming from the depth of the living soul, with heart lifted up above all the heavens, all their powers aflame with burning love, and their spirit raised up into an intelligence empty of images. Here the law of charity is completed, and all virtues are fulfilled. We are emptied, and God, our heavenly Father, dwells in us in the fullness of His grace and we in Him, in a state of fruition and above all our actions. Christ Jesus lives in us, and we in Him: in His life we conquer the world and all sins; and we together with Him are lifted up in love to our heavenly Father. Finally the Holy Spirit works in us, and together with Him, all our good works; He cries within us with a loud voice, yet without words, *Love the love that ever loves you.* His cry is, as it were, an inward touching of our spirit, and His voice more terrible than thunder. The lightnings that break from it lay bare heaven and show us the light and the eternal truth. But such is the heat of this inner touch and of His love, that it would seem to seek to burn us up; and His touch cries in the spirit without ceasing: *Pay your debt. Love the love that ever loves you.* Thence comes a great inward impatience, and an action which can never be complete; for the more we love, the more we long to love; and the more fully we pay the debt that love demands, the deeper in debt we lie. Love is never silent, but ever and without ceasing cries: *Love ye love.*

This contest of love is unknown to those who have not the sense of such things.

The mutual interaction between the love of God and the cessation from His active worship; and the all-sufficing character of the contemplative life

To love and to be fulfilled is to act and be acted upon. God lives in us with His graces; and He teaches, counsels, and commands us to love. But we also live in Him above grace and above our actions when we are acted on by Him and enjoy Him. In us live knowledge, love, contemplation, approach to God; and, above all these, fruition. Our active life consists of loving God: our passive life of receiving the embrace of His love. Between love and fruition is the same relation as between God and His grace. When we cleave to God by love, then we are spirits: but when He takes us out of our spirits and gives us the form of His Spirit, then we are fruition.

And the Spirit of God Himself drives us out, by His breath, to works, love and virtue, and draws us back into Himself for quiet and fruition; and this is eternal life, just as the mortal life of the body subsists by emitting breath and drawing it in anew. And though our spirit may be rapt out of itself, and its activity cease in enjoyment and beatitude, yet it is always renewed in grace, in charity, in virtue. And so, to enter into a restful fruition and go forth again to good works, but ever remain united to the Spirit of God; this is the life of which I wish to tell you. For as we may open our eyes of sense and shut them again so quickly that we feel nothing, so we die in God and live from God and ever live one with God. So we are to go out into the activity of the life of sense, then again go in by love and cleave to God, and remain ever motionless in community with Him. Nor can we feel or comprehend in our spirit anything more excellent than this experience.

Yet we must always be ascending and descending the steps of our heavenly ladder, in interior virtues, outward good works, the commandments of God and the precepts of Holy Church, just as has been said above.

The all-sufficient contemplative life is on the pattern of God's life and is a partaker thereof

And through the likeness of our good works to God, we are united to Him in His fecund nature which ever operates in the trinity of Persons and accomplishes every good thing in the unity of His Spirit. There we are dead to sin in one single spirit with God. There we are born anew of the Holy Spirit, chosen sons of God; there we are rapt in the spirit from ourselves, and the Father with His Son holds us clasped in His eternal love and fruition. And this work is ever new; beginning, operating, and being fulfilled; and herein we are blessed in knowing, loving, and being fulfilled together with God.

In fruition, indeed, we are at rest; for it is only God that acts when He ravishes from themselves His loving spirits, transforms them, and perfects them in the unity of His Spirit. Therein we are all a single fire of love, which is greater than all that was ever created by God. Each single spirit is a glowing coal which God has lit from the flame of His infinite charity; and all of us are gathered up in one burning and inextinguishable fire with the Father and Son in the unity of the Holy Spirit, where even the Divine Persons are, as it were, rapt from themselves in the unity of their essence into a bottomless abyss of simple beatitude. Therein is neither Father nor Son, nor Holy Spirit[132] nor any created thing, but only an eternal essence which is the substance of the Divine Persons. There we are all reunited and created anew; it is our supersubstantial essence. There all fruition is consummated and perfected in essential beatitude. There God is in His simple essence without operation, endless rest, darkness without mode of being, nameless existence, super-essence of all creatures, and an abyssal beatitude of God and all the Saints.

132. One MS. adds at this point 'so far as persons are concerned.' See pp. 4-8 of the Introduction where this and other apparently unorthodox expressions are elucidated.

Furthermore in the fecundity of the divine nature, the Father is one God Almighty, shaper and maker of heaven and earth and all created things. Of His own nature He begets His Son, His Eternal Wisdom, one with Him in nature but distinct in person, God of God, through Whom all things were made. Then from the Father and the Son proceeds in unity of nature the Holy Spirit, third Person of the Trinity. He is the infinite love of both, whereby each in love and fruition eternally embraces the other and also all of us; forming, as it were, but one life, one love, one fruition.

God in unity in nature, trinity in fecundity, three Persons really distinct. These three are unity in nature, but a trinity in Their properties. The fecund nature of God has three properties, which are the three Persons, separate in names and distinction, but one in nature. In operation each single Person has the whole divine nature in Himself; and so each is God omnipotent, in virtue of nature, not distinction of person. The three Persons have also an undivided divine nature and are thereby in nature one God, not three Gods in separation of persons. So therefore God is three names and persons; unity in nature and a trinity in fecundity of nature, which trinity is a property of the Persons, as unity is a property of the nature. And this unity is our Heavenly Father, omnipotent Creator of heaven and earth and all that is. He lives and reigns in us in the highest of our created essence, unity in trinity, trinity in unity, omnipotent God. It is ours to seek, find, and possess Him through His grace and the help of our Lord Jesus Christ, in the Christian faith, with right intention and true charity.

And through our virtuous lives and the grace of God we live in Him and He in us, with all His saints: and so we are all a unity, being made one with Him in love. And the Father and Son have taken hold on us, embraced us and transformed us, in the unity of Their Spirit; and therein we are with the divine Persons one love and one fruition: which fruition is consummated in the divine essence without mode of being. There we are all a simple and essential beatitude with God, and there is neither God nor creature, so far as relates to distinction of persons. There are we all with God, without distinction, beatitude infinite and simple. There we are lost, drowned and liquefied into an unknown darkness.

This is the highest degree of life and of death, of love and of fruition, in eternal beatitude; and whoso teaches otherwise is in error.

Pray for him who has with the grace of God composed and written this, and also for all that shall hear or read it, that God may give Himself to us for life eternal. Amen.

REVELATIONS OF DIVINE LOVE*
By Julian of Norwich

The most optimistic and encouraging mystic that I have read is Julian of Norwich, an Englishwoman of the fourteenth century. Julian believes that she had profound spiritual experiences on the eighth of May 1373. The rest of her life was devoted to meditating the meaning of what she experienced. The following are the written results of some of her meditations.

REVELATIONS OF DIVINE LOVE
God is all that is good, and gently enfolds us;
in comparison with almighty God creation is nothing;
man can have no rest until he totally denies himself
and everything else for love of God

It was at this time that our Lord showed me spiritually how intimately he loves us. I saw that he is everything that we know to be good and helpful. In his love he clothes us, enfolds and embraces us; that tender love completely surrounds us, never to leave us. As I saw it he is everything that is good.

And he showed me more, a little thing, the size of a hazelnut, on the palm of my hand, round like a ball. I looked at it thoughtfully and wondered, 'What is this?' And the answer came, 'It is all that is made.' I marvelled that it continued to exist and did not suddenly disintegrate; it was so small. And again my mind supplied the answer, 'It exists, both now and for ever, because God loves it.' In short, everything owes its existence to the love of God.

In this 'little thing' I saw three truths. The first is that God made it; the second is that God loves it; and the third is that God sustains it. But what he is who is in truth Maker, Keeper, and Lover I cannot tell, for until I am essentially united with him I can never have full rest or real happiness; in other words, until I am so joined to him that there is absolutely nothing between my God and me. We have got to realize the littleness of creation and to see it for the nothing that it is before we can love and possess God who is uncreated. This is the reason why we have no ease of heart or soul, for we are seeking our rest in trivial things which cannot satisfy, and not seeking to know God, almighty, all-wise, all-good. He is true rest. It is his will

---

*Copyright © 1966 by Clifton Wolters. Reprinted by permission of Penguin Books, Ltd., pp. 67-129.

that we should know him, and his pleasure that we should rest in him. Nothing less will satisfy us. No soul can rest until it is detached from all creation. When it is deliberately so detached for love of him who is all, then only can it experience spiritual rest.

God showed me too the pleasure it gives him when a simple soul comes to him, openly, sincerely and genuinely. It seems to me as I ponder this revelation that when the Holy Spirit touches the soul it longs for God rather like this; 'God, of your goodness give me yourself, for you are sufficient for me, I cannot properly ask anything less, to be worthy of you. If I were to ask less, I should always be in want. In you alone do I have all.'

Such words are dear indeed to the soul, and very close to the will and goodness of God. For his goodness enfolds every one of his creatures and all his blessed works, eternally and surpassingly. For he himself is eternity, and has made us for himself alone, has restored us by his blessed passion, and keeps us in his blessed love. And all because he is goodness.

The sharpness of sin; the goodness of contrition; our kind Lord does not wish us to despair over our frequent falls

Sin is the sharpest scourge that any elect soul can be flogged with. It is the scourge which so reduces a man or woman and makes him loathsome in his own sight that it is not long before he thinks himself fit only to sink down to hell ... until the touch of the Holy Spirit forces him to contrition, and turns his bitterness to the hope of God's mercy. Then he begins to heal his wounds, and to rouse his soul as it turns to the life of Holy Church. The Holy Spirit leads him on to confession, so that he deliberately reveals his sins in all their nakedness and reality, and admits with great sorrow and shame that he has befouled the fair image of God. Then for all his sins he performs penance imposed by his confession according to the doctrine of Holy Church, and the teaching of the Holy Spirit. This is one of the humble things that greatly pleases God. Physical illness that is sent by him is another. Others are those humiliations and griefs caused by outside influences, or by the rejection and contempt of the world, or by the various kinds of difficulty and temptation a man may find himself in, whether they be physical or spiritual.

Dearly indeed does our Lord hold on to us when it seems to us that we are nearly forsaken and cast away because of our sin— and deservedly so. Because of the humility we acquire this way we are exalted in the sight of God by his grace, and know a very deep contrition and compassion and a genuine longing for God. Then suddenly we are delivered from sin and pain, and raised to blessedness and even made great saints!

By contrition we are made clean; by compassion, ready; and by a genuine longing for God, worthy. It is by means of these three that souls can attain heaven, as I understand it. (I am referring, of course, to those who were sinners on earth, and who are to be saved.) By these medicines it is necessary for every soul to be healed. Though healed, the soul's wounds are still seen by God, not as wounds, but as honourable scars. Counterbalancing our punishment here with its sorrow and penance is our reward in heaven through the courteous love of almighty God. His will it is that no one getting there shall be deprived of any of the benefits gained by his hardships. For in his lovers he regards sin as a sorrow and a suffering, and, because of his love, not as blameworthy. The reward we will receive will be no small one, but one rather that is great, glorious, and honourable. So shall shame be turned to greater honour and joy.

Our courteous Lord does not want his servants to despair even if they fall frequently and grievously. Our falling does not stop his loving us. Peace and love are always at work in us, but we are not always in peace and love. But he wants us in this way to realize that he is the foundation of the whole of our life in love, and furthermore that he is our eternal protector, and mighty defender against our enemies who are so very fierce and wicked. And, alas, our need is all the greater since we give them every opportunity by our failures.

We must long and love with Jesus, and for love of him
shun sin; sin's vileness exceeds all suffering;
God's tender love for us in our sin;
we need to love our neighbour

It is an expression of royal friendship on the part of our courteous Lord that he holds on to us so tenderly when we are in sin, and that, moreover, his touch is so delicate when he shows us our sin by the gentle light of mercy and grace. When we see our self to be so foul, we know that God is angry with us for our sin. In turn we also are moved by the Holy Spirit to pray contritely, desiring to amend our life to the best of our ability, that we may quench the anger of God and find rest of soul, and an easy conscience. Then we hope that God has forgiven us our sins. And so he has! It is then that our Lord in his courtesy shows himself to the soul, gaily and with cheerful countenance, giving it a friendly welcome as though it had been suffering in prison. 'My beloved,' he says, 'I am glad that you have come to me. In all your trouble I have been with you. Now you can see how I love you. We are made one in blessedness.' So sins are forgiven through merciful grace, and our soul is honourably and joyfully received (just as it will be when it gets to heaven!) whenever it experiences the gracious work of the Holy Spirit, and the virtue of Christ's passion.

By this I know it to be true that all sorts of things are being prepared for us by God's great goodness against that time when we are in peace and in love, and saved in fact. But because it is not possible in this life for us to know this fully, we must endeavour to live with our Lord Jesus in sweet prayer and loving longing. He is always longing to bring us to fullest joy, as was shown earlier when his thirst was revealed.

But if, because of all this spiritual comfort we have been talking of, one were foolish enough to say, 'If this is true, it is a good thing to sin because the reward will be greater,' or to hold sin to be less sinful, then beware! Should such a thought come it would be untrue, and would stem from the enemy of the very love that tells of all this comfort. The same blessed love teaches us that we should hate sin for Love's sake alone. I am quite clear about this: the more a soul sees this in the courtesy of love of our Lord God, the more he hates to sin, and the greater is his sense of shame. For if there could be set before us all the pains of hell, purgatory, earth, death, and so on, on the one hand, and sin on the other, we should choose to have all that pain rather than to sin. For sin is so vile and utterly hateful that no pain can compare with it which is not sin. I was shown no harder hell than sin. The soul by its very nature can have no hell but sin.

When we set our will to be loving and humble the effect of mercy and grace is to make everyone beautiful and clean. As mighty and as wise as God is to save men, so great too is his purpose for us. For Christ himself is the foundation of all the laws by which Christians live, and he taught us to prefer good to evil. He himself exemplifies this love, and practises what he preaches. His will is that we should be entirely like him in our continuing love for ourselves and our fellow Christians. His love for us is not broken by our sins; nor does he intend that our love should be broken for ourselves or our fellow Christians. We are to hate sin absolutely, we are to love the soul eternally, just as God loves it. Our hatred of sin will be like God's hatred of it: our love of the soul like God's. This word he has said is continual comfort: 'I keep you securely.'

The fourteenth revelation: we cannot pray for mercy and not have it; God wills us to pray always, even in aridity; such prayer pleases him

After this our Lord showed me about prayer. The result of this revelation is that I now see that there are two conditions about prayer. One concerns its rightness, the other our sure trust.

Often enough our trust is not wholehearted, for we are not sure that God hears us. We think it is due to our unworthiness and because we feel absolutely nothing: we are often as barren and dry after our prayers as we were before. This awareness of our foolishness is the cause of our weakness. At least, this has been my own experience.

All this our Lord brought immediately to mind, and in this revelation said, 'I am the foundation of your praying. In the first place my will is that you should pray, and then I make it your will too, and since it is I who make you pray, and you do so pray, how can you not have what you ask for?'

Thus in this first reason, and the three that follow, our good Lord showed me great comfort, as can be gathered from his words. In the first reason, when he says 'and you do so pray,' he reveals his great pleasure, and the eternal reward that he gives to us who pray. In the second reason, where he says 'how can you not have?', he is talking of something which is not possible; for it is quite impossible that we should pray for mercy and grace, and not receive it! Everything that our Lord makes us ask for he has ordained for us from before time. So now we can see that it is not our praying that is the cause of God's goodness to us. He showed this to be true in that lovely word, 'I am the foundation.' It is our Lord's will that this truth be known by all his earthly lovers. The more we know it to be true, the more we shall pray, if we are sensible. This is our Lord's meaning.

Prayer is the deliberate act of the soul. It is true, full of grace, and lasting, for it is united with and fixed into the will of our Lord by the inner working of the Holy Spirit. Our Lord himself is the first to receive the prayer—as I see it—and he accepts it gratefully and joyfully. Then he sends it up above, and puts it in the treasury where it will never perish. There it remains continually, before God and his holy ones, ever helping our needs. And when we come to our bliss it shall be given back to us, a contribution to our joy, with his eternal, glorious, gratitude.

Our Lord is greatly cheered by our prayer. He looks for it, and he wants it. By his grace he aims to make us as like himself in heart as we are already in our human nature. This is his blessed will. So he says, 'Pray inwardly, even if you do not enjoy it. It does good, though you feel nothing, see nothing. Yes, even though you think you are doing nothing. For when you are dry, empty, sick, or weak, at such a time is your prayer most pleasing to me though you find little enough to enjoy in it. This is true of all believing prayer.'

Because of the reward and everlasting gratitude he wants us to have, he is eager to see us pray always. God accepts his servant's intention and effort, whatever our feelings. It pleases him that we should work away at our praying and at our Christian living by the help of his grace, and that we consciously direct all our powers to him, until such time as, in all fullness of joy, we have him whom we seek, Jesus. This is the burden of the fifth revelation earlier on, where he says, 'You will have me as your reward.'[133]

With prayer goes gratitude. Thanksgiving is a real, interior, knowledge. With great reverence and loving fear, it turns us with all our powers to do whatever our good Lord indicates. It brings joy and gratitude within. Sometimes its very abundance gives voice, 'Good Lord, thank you and bless you!' And sometimes when the heart is dry and unfeeling—or it may be because of the enemy's tempting—then reason and grace drive us to cry aloud to our Lord, recalling his blessed passion and great goodness. And the strength of our Lord's word comes to the soul, and fires the heart, and leads it by grace into its real business, enabling it to pray happily and to enjoy our Lord in truth. Thanksgiving is a blessed thing in his sight.

133. In fact, these words occur in the fifteenth revelation. But the thought of the present passage is closer to the spirit of the fifth, and though one manuscript corrects 'fifth' to 'fifteenth,' Julian's scribe probably did write 'fifth.'

*The blessed woman saw God in many ways,
but she saw him take his rest nowhere but in man's soul;
his will is that we rejoice more in his love than we
sorrow over our frequent falls, that we remember
the everlasting reward, and live in glad penitence;
why God allows sin*

Our good Lord showed himself to me in various ways both in
heaven and on earth. But the only *place* I saw him occupy was
in man's soul. He showed himself on earth in his precious
incarnation and his blessed passion. In another way he
showed himself—on earth still—when I said 'I saw the whole
Godhead as it were in a single point.' Yet another way was his
showing of himself as being as it were on pilgrimage; in other
words, he is here with us, leading us on, and staying by us until
he has brought us all to his blessedness in heaven. He often
showed himself as reigning, as I have related, but chiefly in
man's soul. There he has made his resting place, and his
glorious city. From this most honoured abode he will never rise
nor remove.

The place of the Lord's dwelling is wonderful and splendid,
so he wants us to respond at once to his gracious touch,
rejoicing in the completeness of his love rather than sorrowing
over our frequent falls. Of all the things we may do for him in
our penitence the most honouring to him is to live gladly and
gaily because of his love. So mercifully does he look on us that
he regards our whole life here as a penance. That deep longing
we have for him is a never ending penance to us; it is a penance
that he produces in us, and one which he mercifully helps us to
bear. His love makes him long for us; his wisdom, truth, and
righteousness enable him to tolerate our being here; and he
wants us to see it this way too. This is a very kind penance, in
my view, and the greatest! It will be with us until such time as
we are made perfect, when we shall possess him as our reward.
And so he wills that we set our heart on that 'pass-over'—over
from the pain we now experience into the bliss we trust in.

*God looks at the soul's grief with pity, not blame;
yet we do nothing but sin; in it we are kept in solace
and fear; God wants us to turn to him, and cling to
his love, and see him to be our medicine; we must love,
in longing and enjoyment; anything opposed to this
comes from the enemy, not God*

But here our courteous Lord showed me our soul mourning and moaning. He explained, 'I know very well that your will is to live loving me, enduring cheerfully and gladly whatever penance may come. But since you do not live without sinning, you are willing to suffer, for love of me, all the distress, trouble, and discomfort that may come. Rightly so. But do not be too perturbed by the sins you commit involuntarily.'

Here I came to understand how the Lord looks at his servant with pity, and not with censure. This passing life does not ask us to live altogether without blame or sin. He loves us eternally—and we sin constantly! He shows us our sin so quietly, and then we are sorry and mourn over each one; we turn to see his mercy, and cling to his love and goodness, for we realize that he is our medicine while we do nothing but sin. So, humbled by the sight of our sin, and knowing and trusting his love, we thank him and praise him and please him. 'I love you, and you love me,' he has said 'and our love will never be broken. For your sake I suffer these things.' All this was shown to my spirit's understanding when these blessed words were said, 'I will keep you safe and sound.'

By the great desire I have in our blessed Lord that we should live this way—longing and rejoicing, as this lesson on love shows—I understood that all impediments come not from him but from the enemy. He wills us to know this through the gracious and sweet light of his kindly love. Should there be anywhere one of his lovers who is forever kept from falling I know nothing about it: it was not shown me. But this was shown: both when we fall and when we get up again we are kept in the same precious love. In God's sight we do not fall: in our own we do not stand. I see both of these to be true. But God's sight is the higher truth. We are deeply indebted to him that he should want to show us this great truth here below. I saw that it is a very great help for us to see both these truths at one and the same time while we are alive here. The higher, 'God's sight,' comforts us spiritually in him, and gives us true enjoyment; the other, more lowly, sight keeps us fearful and ashamed. But our good Lord wants us always to pay more attention to the higher, while not neglecting all knowledge of the lower, until the time we are brought to heaven, where our reward will be the Lord Jesus, and we shall be filled with joy and bliss for ever.

Three attributes of God; life, love, and light;
our reason agrees; it is God's greatest gift;
our faith is a light which comes from the Father;
it is measured to our need, and leads us through the
night; at the end of our troubles our eyes will be
opened suddenly; this full light and clarity is God
our Maker, Father, and Holy Spirit,
through Jesus, our Savior

I had, in some measure, both touch, sight, and feeling of three of God's attributes, and on them the strength and effectiveness of the whole revelation depends. They occur in every revelation, and particularly in the twelfth where it is often said, 'It is I.' The attributes are these: life, love, and light. In 'life' there is this marvellous intimacy, and in 'love' that gentle courtesy, and in 'light' our everlasting nature. These three exist in one goodness; to which goodness my own reason would be united, holding on to it with all its power. I gazed with reverence and fear, greatly wondering both at the sight itself and at the feeling of sweet harmony that our reason should be in God. I knew it was the greatest gift we have ever received, and one that was based in our nature.

Our faith is a light, coming to us naturally from him who is our everlasting Day, our Father, and our God. By this light Christ, our Mother, and the Holy Spirit, our good Lord, lead us through these passing years. The light is measured to our individual needs as we face our night. Because of the light we live: because of the night we suffer and grieve. Through this grief we earn reward and thanks from God. With the help of mercy and grace, we know and trust our light quite deliberately, and with it we go forward intelligently and firmly. When we are done with grief our eyes will be suddenly enlightened, and in the shining brightness of the light we shall see perfectly. For our light is none other than God our Maker, and the Holy Spirit, in our Savior, Christ Jesus.

So did I see and understand that faith is our light in darkness, and our light is God, the everlasting Day.

What prayer effects when in line with God's will;
God's goodness delights in his deeds done through us,
as though he were indebted to us;
all things work sweetly

Prayer unites the soul to God. However like God the soul may be in essence and nature (once it has been restored by grace), it is often unlike him in fact because of man's sin. Then it is that prayer proclaims that the soul should will what God wills; and it strengthens the conscience and enables a man to obtain grace. God teaches us to pray thus, and to trust firmly that we shall have what we ask. For he looks at us in love, and would have us share in his good work. So he moves us to pray for what it is he wants to do. For such prayer and good will—and it is his gift—he rewards us eternally. And the word 'and you do so pray' shows all this. In it God takes as great pleasure and delight as if he were indebted to us for all the good we do. And yet it is he who actually does it! Because we pray earnestly that he should do whatever he wills, it is as though he said, 'What can please me more than to have you pray fervently, wisely, and earnestly to do what I am going to do?' So does the soul by prayer conform to God.

But when our Lord in his courtesy and grace shows himself to our soul we have what we desire. Then we care no longer about praying for any thing, for our whole strength and aim is set on beholding. This is prayer, high and ineffable, in my eyes. The whole reason why we pray is summed up in the sight and vision of him to whom we pray. Wondering, enjoying, worshipping, fearing . . . and all with such sweetness and delight that during that time we can only pray in such ways as he leads us. Well do I know that the more the soul sees God, the more by his grace does it want him.

But when we do not see him thus, we feel the more need to pray to Jesus because of our basic failure and incapacity. For when the soul is tossed and troubled and alone in its unrest, it is time to pray so as to make itself sensitive and submissive to God. Of course prayer cannot in any way make God sensitive to the soul: for this is what, in his love, he always is. And I realized, moreover, that when we know we have got to pray, then our good Lord follows this up, helping our desire. And when by his special grace we see him clearly, there is need of nothing further. We have to follow him, drawn by his love into himself. For I saw and knew that this marvellous and utter goodness brings our powers up to their full strength. At the same time I saw that he is at work unceasingly in every conceivable thing, and that it is all done so well, so wisely, and so powerfully that it is far greater than anything we can imagine, guess, or think. Then we can do no more than gaze in delight with a tremendous desire to be wholly united to him, to live where he lives, to enjoy his love, and to delight in his goodness. It is then that we, through our humble, persevering prayer, and the help of his grace, come to him now, in this present life. There will be many secret touches that we shall feel and see, sweet and spiritual, and adapted to our ability to receive them. This is achieved by the grace of the Holy Spirit, both now and until the time that, still longing and loving, we die. On that day we shall come to our Lord knowing our self clearly, possessing God completely.

THE COMPLETE WORKS OF
ST. JOHN OF THE CROSS*
Trans. and edited by E. Allison Peers

St. John, a giant in the field of mysticism, and the spiritual friend of St. Teresa, has already been introduced. John was a poet as well as a mystic. The following excerpt is one of his poems of mystic ecstasy. The last stanza is interpreted by a commentary.

THE COMPLETE WORKS OF
ST. JOHN OF THE CROSS
Songs of the soul in the intimate communion of the union of the love of God. By the same author.

1. O living flame of love
   That, burning, dost assail
   My inmost soul with tenderness untold,
   Since thou dost freely move,
   Deign to consume the veil
   Which sunders this sweet converse that we hold.

2. O burn that searest never!
   O wound of deep delight!
   O gentle hand! O touch of love supernal
   That quick'nest life for ever,
   Putt'st all my woes to flight,
   And, slaying, changest death to life eternal!

3. And O, ye lamps of fire,
   In whose resplendent light
   The deepest caverns where the senses meet,
   Once steep'd in darkness dire,
   Blaze with new glories bright
   And to the lov'd one give both light and heat!

4. How tender is the love
   Thou wak'nest in my breast
   When thou, alone and secretly, art there!
   Whispering of things above,
   Most glorious and most blest,
   How delicate the love thou mak'st me bear!

*Reprinted from *The Complete Works of St. John of the Cross*, translated and edited by E. Allison Peers. Westminster, Maryland, Newman, 1964, Vol. II, pp. 424, 425; Vol. III pp. 187-195. Used with permission of Search Press, London.

STANZA IV

How gently and lovingly thou awakenest in my bosom,
Where thou dwellest secretly and alone!
And in thy sweet breathing, full of blessing and glory,
How delicately thou inspirest my love!

Exposition

Here the soul turns to its Spouse with great love, extolling Him and giving Him thanks for two wondrous effects which He sometimes produces within it by means of this union, noting likewise in what way He produces each and also the effect upon itself which in each case is the result thereof.

The first effect is the awakening of God in the soul, and the means whereby this is produced are those of gentleness and love. The second effect is the breathing of God in the soul and the means thereof are in the blessing and glory that are communicated to the soul in this breathing. And that which is produced thereby in the soul is a delicate and tender inspiration of love.

The stanza, then, has this meaning: Thine awakening, O Word and Spouse, in the centre and depth of my soul, which is its pure and inmost substance, wherein alone, secretly and in silence, Thou dwellest as its only Lord, not only as in Thine own house, nor even as in Thine own bed, but intimately and closely united as in mine own bosom—how gentle and how loving is this![134] That is, it is exceedingly gentle and loving; and in this delectable breathing which Thou makest in this Thine awakening, delectable for me, filled as it is with blessing and glory, with what delicacy dost Thou inspire me with love and affection for Thyself! Herein the soul uses a similitude of the breathing of one that awakens from his sleep; for in truth, the soul in this condition feels it to be so. There follows the line:

How gently and lovingly thou awakenest in my bosom,

There are many ways in which God awakens in the soul: so many that, if we had to begin to enumerate them, we should never end. But this awakening of the Son of God which the soul here desires to describe, is, as I believe, one of the loftiest and one which brings the greatest good to the soul. For this awakening is a movement of the Word in the substance of the soul, of such greatness and dominion and glory, and of such intimate sweetness,[135] that it seems to the soul that all the

---

134. Bg, P: 'is this awakening!'
135. Bz: 'such immense sweetness.' C: 'such great sweetness.'

balms and perfumed spices and flowers in the world are mingled and shaken and revolved together to give their sweetness; and that all the kingdoms and dominions of the world and all the powers[136] and virtues of Heaven are moved. And not only so, but all the virtues and substances and perfections and graces of all created things shine forth and make the same movement together and in unison. For, as Saint John says,[137] all things in Him are life, and in Him they live and are and move, as the Apostle says likewise.[138] Hence it comes to pass that, when this great Emperor moves in the soul, Whose kingdom, as Isaias says, is borne upon His shoulder[139] (namely, the three spheres, the celestial, the terrestrial and the infernal, and the things that are in them; and He sustains them all, as Saint Paul says, with the Word of His virtue)[140] then all the spheres seem to move together. Just as, when the earth moves, all material things that are upon it move likewise, as if they were nothing, even so, when this Prince moves, He carries His court with Him, and the court carries not Him.

Yet this comparison is highly unsuitable, for in this latter case not only do all seem to be moving, but they also reveal the beauties of their being, virtue, loveliness and graces, and the root of their duration[141] and life. For there the soul is able to see how all creatures, above and below, have their life and strength and duration in Him, and it sees clearly that which the Book of the Proverbs expresses in these words: 'By Me kings reign, by Me princes rule and the powerful exercise justice and understand it.'[142] And although it is true that the soul is now able to see that these things are distinct from God, inasmuch as they have a created being, and it sees them in Him, with their force, root and strength, it knows equally that God, in His own Being, is all these things, in an infinite and pre-eminent way,[143] to such a point that it understands them better in His Being than in themselves. And this is the great delight of this awakening: to know the creatures through God and not God through the creatures; to know the effects through their cause and not the cause through the effects; for the latter knowledge is secondary and this other is essential.

136. Bg, P: 'all the creatures, powers.'
137. St. John i, 3.
138. Acts xvii, 28.
139. Isaias ix, 6.
140. Hebrews i, 3.
141. Bz: 'detraction.'
142. Proverbs viii, 15.
143. [*Lit.,* 'with infinite eminence.'] S: 'with infinite immensity.'

And the manner of this movement[144] in the soul, since God is immovable, is a wondrous thing, for, although in reality God moves not, it seems to the soul that He is indeed moving; for, as it is the soul that is renewed and moved[145] by God it may behold this supernatural sight, and there is revealed to it in this great renewal that Divine life and the being and harmony of all creatures[146] in it which have their movements in God, it seems to the soul that it is God that is moving, and thus the cause takes the name of the effect which it produces, according to which effect we may say that God is moving, even as the Wise Man says: 'Wisdom is more movable than all movable things.'[147] And this is not because it moves itself, but because it is the beginning and root of all movement; remaining in itself stable, as the passage goes on to say, it renews all things. And thus what is here meant is that wisdom is more active than all active things. And thus we should say here that it is the soul that is moved in this motion, and is awakened from the sleep of its natural vision to a supernatural vision, for which reason it is very properly given the name of an awakening.

But God, as the soul is enabled to see, is always moving, ruling and giving being and virtue and graces and gifts to all creatures, containing them all in Himself, virtually, presentially and substantially; so that in one single glance the soul sees that which God is in Himself and that which He is in His creatures. Even so, when a palace is thrown open, a man may see at one and the same time the eminence of the person who is within the palace and also what he is doing. And it is this, as I understand it, that happens upon this awakening and glance of the soul. Though the soul is substantially in God, as is every creature, He draws back from before it some of the veils and curtains which are in front of it, so that it may see of what nature He is; and then there is revealed to it, and it is able to see[148] (though somewhat darkly, since not all the veils are drawn back) that face of His that is full of graces. And, since it is moving all things by its power, there appears together with it that which it is doing, and it appears to move in them, and they in it, with continual movement; and for this reason the soul believes that God has moved and awakened, whereas in reality that which has moved and awakened is itself.

144. Bz, C: 'knowledge.'
145. Bz: 'is moved and guided.'
146. Bg, P: 'of all things and creatures.'
147. Wisdom vii, 24. Bz has 'causes' for 'things.'
148. Bz: 'to descry.'

For such is the lowly nature of this kind of life which we live[149] that we believe others to be as we are ourselves; and we judge others as we are ourselves, so that our judgment proceeds from ourselves and begins with ourselves and not outside ourselves. In this way the thief believes that others steal likewise; and he that lusts, that others also are lustful like himself;[150] and he that bears malice, that others bear malice, his judgment proceeding from his own malice; and the good man thinks well of others, his judgment proceeding from the goodness of his own thoughts; and so likewise he that is negligent and slothful thinks that others are the same. And hence, when we are negligent and slothful in the sight of God, we think that it is God Who is slothful and negligent with us, as we read in the forty-third Psalm, where David says to God:[151] 'Arise, Lord, why sleepest Thou?'[152] He attributes to God qualities that are in man; for though it is they that are asleep and have fallen, yet it is God Whom he bids arise and awaken, though He that keepeth Israel never sleeps.

But in truth, though every blessing that comes to man is from God, and man, of his own power, can do naught that is good, it is true to say that our awakening is an awakening of God, and our uprising is an uprising of God. And thus it is as though David had said: Raise us up and raise us up again[153] and awaken us, for we are asleep and we have fallen in two ways. Wherefore, since the soul had fallen into a sleep, whence of itself it could never awaken, and it is God alone that has been able to open its eyes and cause this awakening, it very properly describes it as an awakening of God, in these words: 'Thou awakenest in my bosom.' Do Thou awaken us, then, and enlighten us, my Lord, that we may know and love the blessings that Thou has ever set before us, and we shall know that Thou has been moved to grant us favours, and that Thou has been mindful of us.

That which the soul knows and feels in this awakening concerning the excellence of God is wholly indescribable, for, since there is a communication of the excellence of God in the substance of the soul, which is that breast of the soul whereof the lines here speak, there is heard in the soul an immense power in the voice of a multitude of excellences, of thousands

149. Bz: 'of our consideration.'
150. S: 'that others are of his condition.'
151. Bg adds: 'in our name.'
152. Psalm xliii, 23 [A.V., xliv, 23].
153. [*Lit.*, 'Raise us up twice.']

upon thousands[154] of virtues of God, which can never be numbered. In these the soul is entrenched and remains terribly and firmly arrayed among them like ranks of armies and made sweet and gracious in all the sweetnesses and graces of the creatures.

But this question will be raised: How can the soul bear so violent[155] a communication while in the weakness of the flesh, when indeed there is no means and strength in it to suffer so greatly without fainting away, since the mere sight of King Assuerus on his throne, in his royal apparel and adorned with gold and precious stones, caused Queen Esther such great fear when she saw how terrible he was to behold that she fainted away, as she confesses in that place where she says she fainted away by reason of the fear caused by his great glory, since he seemed to her like an angel and his face was full of grace.[156] For glory oppresses him that looks upon it if it glorifies him not. And how much more should the soul faint here, since it is no angel that it sees, but God, Whose face is full of graces of all the creatures and of terrible power and glory and Whose voice is the multitude of His excellences? Concerning this Job enquires, when we have such difficulty in hearing a spark, who shall be able to abide the greatness of His thunder.[157] And elsewhere he says: 'I will not that He contend and treat me with much strength, lest perchance He oppress me with the weight of His greatness.'[158]

But the reason why the soul faints not away and fears not in this awakening which is so powerful and glorious is twofold. First, being, as it now is, in the state of perfection, wherein its lower part is thoroughly purged and conformed with the spirit, it feels not the suffering and pain that are wont to be experienced in spiritual communications by spirit and sense when these are not purged and prepared to receive them; although this suffices not to prevent the soul from suffering when it is faced with such greatness and glory; since, although its nature be very pure, yet it will be corrupted because it exceeds nature, even as a physical faculty is corrupted by any sensible thing which exceeds its power, in which sense must be taken that which we quoted from Job. But the second reason is the more revelant: it is that which the soul gave in the first

154. P, S: 'of thousands.' Bz: 'of millions upon thousands.'
155. [*Lit.*, 'so strong.']
156. Esther xv, 16.
157. Job xxvi, 14. P: 'of His face.'
158. Job xxiii, 6.

line—namely, that God shows Himself gentle.[159] For, just as God shows the soul greatness[160] and glory in order to comfort and magnify it, just so does He grant it grace so that it receives no suffering, and protect its nature, showing the spirit His greatness, with tenderness and love, without the natural senses perceiving this, so that the soul knows not if it is in the body or out of the body. This may easily be done by that God Who protected Moses with His right hand that he might see His glory. And thus the soul feels the gentleness and lovingness of God proportionately to His power and dominion and greatness, since in God all these things are one and the same. And thus the delight of the soul is strong, and the protection given to it is strong in gentleness and love, so that it may be able to endure the strength of this delight; and thus the soul, far from fainting away, becomes strong and powerful. For, when Esther swooned, this was because the King showed himself to her at first unfavourably; for, as we read in that place, he showed her his burning eyes and the fury of his breast. But when he looked favourably upon her, stretching out his sceptre[161] and touching her with it and embracing her, she returned to herself, for he had said to her that he was her brother and she was not to fear.

And thus, when the King of Heaven has shown Himself as a friend to the soul, as its equal and its brother, the soul is no longer afraid; for when, in gentleness and not in wrath, He shows to it the strength of His power and the love of His goodness, He communicates to it the strength and love of His breast, and comes out to it from the throne (which is the soul) even as a spouse from his bridal chamber where he was hidden. He inclines to the soul, touches it with the sceptre of His majesty and embraces it as a brother. The soul beholds the royal apparel and perceives its fragrance—namely, the wondrous virtues of God; it observes the spendour of gold, which is charity; it sees the glittering of the precious stones, which are knowledge of created substances, both higher and lower; it looks upon the face of the Word, which is full of graces that strike this queen (which is the soul) and likewise clothe her, so that she may be transformed in these virtues of the King of Heaven and see herself a queen indeed, and thus she may say of herself truly that which David says in the Psalm, namely: 'The queen stood at Thy right hand in apparel of gold

159. Bg adds: 'kind and loving.'
160. Bg: 'this greatness.'
161. Bz: 'his wand.'

and surrounded with variety.[162] And, since all this comes to pass in the inmost substance of the soul, it adds next:

Where thou dwellest secretly and alone!

The soul says that He dwells secretly in its breast, because, as we have said, this sweet embrace is made in the depth of the substance of the soul. That is to say that God dwells secretly in all souls and is hidden in their substance; for, were this not so, they would be unable to exist. But there is a difference between these two manners of dwelling, and a great one. For in some He dwells alone, and in others He dwells not alone; in some He dwells contented and in others He dwells displeased; in some He dwells as in His house, ordering it and ruling everything, while in others He dwells as a stranger in the house of another where He is not allowed to do anything or to give any commands. Where He dwells with the greatest content and most completely alone is in the soul wherein dwell fewest desires and pleasures of its own; here He is in His own house and rules and governs it. The more completely alone does He dwell in the soul, the more secretly He dwells; and thus in this soul wherein dwells no desire, neither any other image or form or affection of aught that is created, the Beloved dwells most secretly, with more intimate, more interior and closer embrace, according as the soul, as we say, is the more purely and completely withdrawn from all save God. And thus He dwells secretly, since the devil cannot attain to this place and to this embrace, neither can the understanding of any man attain to a knowledge of the manner thereof. But He dwells not secretly with respect to the soul which is in this state of perfection, for it feels[163] this intimate embrace within it. Yet this is not always so, for, when the Beloved causes these awakenings to take place, it seems to the soul that He is awakening in its bosom, where aforetime He was, as it were, sleeping; for, although it felt and enjoyed His presence, it experienced it as that of the Beloved asleep in its bosom;[164] and, when one of two persons is asleep, the understanding and love of them both are not mutually communicated, nor can they be until both have awakened.

Oh, how happy is this soul that is ever conscious of God resting and reposing within its breast! Oh, how well is it that it

162. Psalm xliv, 10.
163. Bg: 'which ever feels.'
164. Bz, C, S: 'the Beloved sleeping in slumber.'

should withdraw from all things, flee from business and live in boundless tranquillity, lest anything, however small,[165] or the slightest turmoil should disturb or turn away[166] the bosom of the Beloved within it. He is there, habitually, as it were, asleep in this embrace with the bride, in the substance of the soul; and of this the soul is quite conscious, and habitually has fruition of Him, for, if He were for ever awake[167] within it, communicating knowledge and love to it, it would be already living in glory. For, if one single awakening of God within the soul, and one glance from His eye, set it in such bliss, as we have said, what would its condition be if He were habitually within it and it were conscious of His being awake?[168]

In other souls, that have not attained to this union, He dwells secretly likewise; and He is not displeased, since after all they are in grace, though they are not yet perfectly prepared for union. Such souls are not as a rule conscious of His presence save when He effects certain delectable awakenings within them, but these are not of the same kind or quality as that other awakening, nor have they aught to do with it. This awakening is not so secret from the understanding, or from the devil, as that other,[169] for something can always be understood concerning it by means of the movements of sense, inasmuch as sense is not completely annihilated until the soul attains to union, but still preserves certain actions and movements pertaining to the spiritual element, for it is not yet absolutely and wholly spiritualized. But in this awakening which the Spouse effects in this perfect soul, everything that happens and is done is perfect; for it is He that is its sole cause. Thus it is as if[170] a man awakened and breathed; the soul is conscious of a rare delight in the breathing of the Holy Spirit in God, in Whom it is glorified and enkindled in love Therefore it utters the lines following:

And in thy sweet breathing, full of blessing and glory,
How delicately thou inspirest my love!

Of that breathing of God, which is full of blessing and glory and of the delicate love of God for the soul, I should not wish to

165. [*Lit.,* 'lest the very smallest speck,' a stronger expression than in the first redaction.] Bg, Bz read '[manifestation of] knowledge' [*noticia*]. P reads 'sign.'
166. Bg: 'or move.'
167. Bg: 'awakening.'
168. [*Lit.,* 'within it, for it well awake.'] Bg, Bz: 'for it well prepared.'
169. Bg, Bz, P have confused renderings of this passage. Bz also reads: 'the understanding of man,' and Bg, P: 'another's understanding.'
170. Bg: 'And then that aspiration and awakening are as if.'

speak, neither do I desire now to speak; for I see clearly that I cannot say aught concerning it, and that, were I to speak of it, it would not appear as great as it is.[171] For it is a breathing of God Himself into the soul, wherein, through that awakening of lofty knowledge of the Deity, the Holy Spirit breathes into the soul according to the understanding and knowledge which it has had of God, wherein He most profoundly absorbs it in the Holy Spirit, Who inspires it with Divine delicacy and glory, according to that which it has seen in God; for, His breathing being full of blessing and glory, the Holy Spirit has filled the soul with blessing and glory, wherein He has inspired it with love for Himself, which transcends all description and all sense, in the deep things of God, to Whom be[172] honour and glory. Amen.[173]

171. So Bg, P. The other authorities [followed by P. Silverio] read: 'it would appear that it is.'
172. Bg, P: 'be given.'
173. So S. Bg, C, P: 'and glory *in soecula soeculorum*. Amen.' Bz: 'and glory in the ages of the ages. Amen.' Bg, P add: '*Laus Deo.*'